# Literature
### of the
# American
# Southwest

PRENTICE HALL
Upper Saddle River, New Jersey
Needham, Massachusetts

ISBN 0-13-435449-4

5 6 7 8 9 10    02 01 00

PRENTICE HALL

# Acknowledgments

Grateful acknowledgment is made to the following for copyrighted material:

**Arte Publico Press**

"The Sense of Place" by Rolando Hinojosa, from *The Rolando Hinojosa Reader*, edited by Jose David Saldivar. (Houston: Arte Publico Press/University of Houston, 1985). "Señora X No More" from *Communion* by Pat Mora (Houston: Arte Publico Press/University of Houston, 1991). "Picture of His Father's Face" by Tomás Rivera, translated by Rolando Hinojosa, from *This Migrant Earth* (Houston: Arte Publico Press/University of Houston, 1987). Reprinted with permission from the publisher.

**Susan Bergholz Literary Services**

"Salvador Late or Early" from *Woman Hollering Creek*. Copyright © 1991 by Sandra Cisneros. Published by Vintage Books, a division of Random House, Inc., and originally in hardcover by Random House, Inc. Reprinted by permission of Susan Bergholz Literary Services, New York. All rights reserved.

**Harcourt Brace & Company**

"He" from *Flowering Judas and Other Stories*, copyright 1930 and renewed 1958 by Katherine Anne Porter, reprinted by permission of Harcourt Brace & Company.

**Journal of Southern History (Southern Historical Association)**

"The Importance of Dancing to Early Texans" from *Amusements in the Republic of Texas* by William Ransom Hogan, reprinted from *The Journal of Southern History*, Vol. III, No. 4, November, 1937. Copyright 1938 by the Southern Historical Association. Reprinted by permission.

**Museum of New Mexico Press**

"The Deer Thief" and "The Parrot Who Bought Firewood" from *Cuentos: Tales from the Hispanic Southwest*, selected by and adapted in Spanish by Jose Griego y Maestas, retold in English by Rudolfo A. Anaya. Copyright © 1980 by The Museum of New Mexico Press.

*(Acknowledgments continue on p. 121.)*

# Contents

# Introduction

The southwestern United States has a colorful history and a rich cultural heritage. In this anthology, you'll encounter folk tales, stories, essays, and poems that reflect the exciting past and give voice to the many cultures—Native American, Mexican, European, and American—that make this region unique.

The anthology opens with two *cuentos*—traditional tales from the Hispanic Southwest—retold by Rudolfo Anaya. One tells of a man who uses his wits to catch a thief, and another describes a precocious parrot. Also included in this section are a pair of tall tales, one describing a braggart from Arkansas and the other, a story from the early life of the legendary Pecos Bill.

The short-story section begins with Katherine Anne Porter's "He," a poignant story by one of the most acclaimed writers from Texas. The work of modern-day Texans is also included: an excerpt from the novel *Lonesome Dove* by Larry McMurtry and coming-of-age stories by Robert Flynn and Sandra Cisneros. Fiction by Luci Tapahonso, Tomás Rivera, and Diana García completes this section of the anthology.

The first nonfiction entry in the anthology is a short account of the 1540 expedition by Spanish explorer Francisco Vásquez de Coronado to what is now New Mexico. This historical narrative is told by Pedro de Castañeda, who lived in northwestern Mexico at the time of Coronado's journey. Other historical pieces include an 1832 petition encouraging residents of Mexico to emigrate to Texas, diary entries from a young woman who traveled the Santa Fe Trail, and a riveting first-person account of the battle of the Alamo by a survivor who was only a boy at the time of the siege. The section ends with contemporary nonfiction selections: Bryan Woolley's commentary on the tourist attraction that the Alamo has become today and a humorous account of a southwestern town rich in oil, yet sorely in need of clean drinking water.

The final section of the anthology features the poetry of southwestern writers. Selections range from a traditional Navajo chant to childhood reminiscences by Naomi Shihab Nye and Tino Villanueva. Works by other acclaimed poets—such as Pat Mora, Leslie Marmon Silko, Simon Ortiz, and Joy Harjo—are also included.

As you read this anthology, you will find that although the selections vary greatly in terms of genre, time period, and writer's background, they all share the flavor and spirit of the American Southwest.

# The Deer Thief

## Retold by Rudolfo A. Anaya

A hunter was out hunting one day and killed a deer. Since it was very late in the day he couldn't take the deer home, so he skinned it and hung it as high as he could from the branch of a tall pine tree. The following day he returned for his deer, but the deer was gone. He searched the area for tracks. He inspected everything very carefully, and then he went to the Justice of the Peace to seek redress.

The Justice of the Peace asked him if he had any idea who stole the deer. The hunter replied that he had not seen the thief and he didn't know who it was, but he could give an accurate description of the man who stole the deer.

"If you know something, tell me what kind of man he is," the Justice of the Peace said.

"Well, he is shorter than I. He is older, and he had a yellow bulldog with him."

"But how do you know all that?"

"I know he is shorter than I because he had to put some logs beneath the tree to reach the deer," replied the hunter.

"And how do you know he is old?"

"Because he took short steps, like an old man."

"And how do you know he had a yellow dog?"

"I followed his tracks and I found yellow hair where the dog passed beneath low branches."

"But how do you know it was a bulldog?" the exasperated judge asked.

"Because when the old man was lowering the deer, the dog sat nearby and the way the stub of his tail dug into the ground told me it was a bulldog."

The judge was convinced and granted permission to look for a man fitting that description. After searching for some time the hunter and the Justice of the Peace arrived at a house where they saw a yellow bulldog. They knocked on the door and a small, old man appeared. Then they searched his barn and found the stolen deer. So the hunter, by using his wits, had tracked down the thief who had stolen his deer.

# The Parrot Who Bought Firewood

## Retold by Rudolfo A. Anaya

WHEN the first snow powdered the Sangre de Cristo Mountains and the cold winds whistled through the valley and froze the Santa Fe River, the men who sold firewood would load their burros with wood and go through the streets of Santa Fe selling wood.

One day two wood vendors passed by the plaza and stopped near the house of a man who bought from them regularly. Now it so happened that no one was home, but the woman of the house had a parrot who spoke many words in Spanish.

The parrot had seen and heard his master buy firewood many times before, so when the vendors called, *"Leña, leña para vender!"* the parrot whistled and answered, *"Si, compro leña!"*— Yes, I'll buy some firewood!

The vendors thought it was the master of the house who had shouted out that he wanted firewood, so they unloaded their burros at the woodpile. But when they went to collect for the wood no one answered the door, so they decided to return that afternoon for their pay.

When the master of the house and his wife returned from their visitations around the Royal City they saw the fresh wood. Shortly thereafter the woodsmen came for their pay.

"But I didn't buy firewood," the master of the house said.

"Someone shouted from the house that you needed wood," the vendors insisted.

Then the woman remembered that she had left the parrot out of his cage, and she suspected that he had been the one who had bought the wood. So they paid for the firewood, and the woman scolded the parrot who then sulked off down to the cellar.

Meanwhile, the cat climbed up on the table and took a piece of the meat the man had bought in town. When the woman saw what the cat had done she turned to punish him and threw him into the cellar.

When the parrot saw the cat tossed into the cellar for his misdeed, he chuckled and said, "What happened? Did you buy firewood too?"

# The Big Bear of Arkansas

## T. B. Thorpe

A steamboat on the Mississippi frequently, in making her regular trips, carries between places varying from one to two thousand miles apart; and as these boats advertise to land passengers and freight at "all intermediate landings," the heterogeneous
character of the passengers of one of these up-country boats can
scarcely be imagined by one who has never seen it with his own
eyes. Starting from New Orleans in one of these boats, you will
find yourself associated with men from every state in the Union,
and from every portion of the globe; and a man of observation
need not lack for amusement or instruction in such a crowd, if he
will take the trouble to read the great book of character so favour-
ably opened before him. Here may be seen jostling together the
wealthy Southern planter, and the pedlar of tin-ware from New
England—the Northern merchant, and the Southern jockey—a
venerable bishop, and a desperate gambler—the land speculator,
and the honest farmer—professional men of all creeds and characters—Wolvereens, Suckers, Hoosiers, Buckeyes, and Corn-
crackers, beside a "plentiful sprinkling" of the half-horse and half-
alligator species of men, who are peculiar to "old Mississippi," and
who appear to gain a livelihood simply by going up and down the
river. In the pursuit of pleasure or business, I have frequently
found myself in such a crowd.

On one occasion, when in New Orleans, I had occasion to
take a trip of a few miles up the Mississippi, and I hurried on
board the well-known "high-pressure-and-beat-every-thing"
steamboat *Invincible,* just as the last note of the last bell was
sounding; and when the confusion and bustle that is natural to
a boat's getting under way had subsided, I discovered that I was
associated in as heterogeneous a crowd as was ever got together. As my trip was to be of a few hours' duration only, I
made no endeavours to become acquainted with my fellow passengers, most of whom would be together many days. Instead of
this, I took out of my pocket the "latest paper," and more criti-
cally than usual examined its contents; my fellow passengers at
the same time disposed themselves in little groups. While I was
thus busily employed in reading, and my companions were
more busily employed in discussing such subjects as suited

3

their humours best, we were startled most unexpectedly by a loud Indian whoop, uttered in the "social hall," that part of the cabin fitted off for a bar; then was to be heard a loud crowing, which would not have continued to have interested us—such sounds being quite common in that place of spirits—had not the hero of these windy accomplishments stuck his head into the cabin and hallooed out, "Hurra for the Big Bar of Arkansaw!" and then might be heard a confused hum of voices, unintelligible, save in such broken sentences as "horse," "screamer," "lightning is slow," &c. As might have been expected, this continued interruption attracted the attention of every one in the cabin; all conversation dropped, and in the midst of this surprise the "Big Bar" walked into the cabin, took a chair, put his feet on the stove, and looking back over his shoulder, passed the general and familiar salute of "Strangers, how are you?" He then expressed himself as much at home as if he had been at "the Forks of Cypress," and "perhaps a little more so." Some of the company at this familiarity looked a little angry, and some astonished; but in a moment every face was wreathed in a smile. There was something about the intruder that won the heart on sight. He appeared to be a man enjoying perfect health and contentment; His eyes were as sparkling as diamonds, and good-natured to simplicity. Then his perfect confidence in himself was irresistibly droll. "Perhaps," said he, "gentlemen," running on without a person speaking, "perhaps you have been to New Orleans often; I never made *the first visit before,* and I don't intend to make another in a crow's life. I am thrown away in that ar place, and useless, that ar a fact. Some of the gentlemen thar called me *green*—well, perhaps I am, said I, *but I arn't so at home;* and if I ain't off my trail much, the heads of them perlite chaps themselves wern't much the hardest; for according to my notion, they were real *know-nothings,* green as a pumpkin-vine—couldn't, in farming, I'll bet, raise a crop of turnips: and as for shooting, they'd miss a barn if the door was swinging, and that, too, with the best rifle in the country. And then they talked to me 'bout hunting, and laughed at my calling the principal game in Arkansaw poker, and high-low-jack. 'Perhaps,' said I, 'you prefer chickens and rolette'; at this they laughed harder than ever, and asked me if I lived in the woods, and didn't know what *game* was? At this I rather think I laughed. 'Yes,' I roared, and says, 'Strangers, if you'd asked me *how we got our meat* in Arkansaw, I'd a told you at once, and given you a list of varmints that would make a caravan, beginning with the bar, and ending off with the cat; that's *meat* though, not game.' Game, indeed, that's what city folks call it; and with them it means chippen-birds and shite-pokes; maybe such trash live in my diggens, but I arn't noticed them yet: a bird any way is too trifling. I never did shoot at but one, and I'd never forgiven myself for that, had it weighed less than forty pounds. I wouldn't draw a rifle on any thing less than that; and when I meet with another wild turkey of the same weight I will drap him."

"A wild turkey weighing forty pounds!" exclaimed twenty voices in the cabin at once.

"Yes, strangers, and wasn't it a whopper? You see, the thing was so fat that it couldn't fly far; and when he fell out of the tree, after I shot him, on striking the ground he bust open behind, and the way the pound gobs of tallow rolled out of the opening was perfectly beautiful."

"Where did all that happen?" asked a cynical-looking Hoosier.

"Happen! happened in Arkansaw: where else could it have happened, but in the creation state, the finishing-up country—a state where the *sile* runs down to the centre of the 'arth, and government gives you a title to every inch of it? Then its airs—just breathe them, and they will make you snort like a horse. It's a state without a fault, it is."

"Excepting mosquitoes," cried the Hoosier.

"Well, stranger, except them; for it ar a fact that they ar rather *enormous*, and do push themselves in somewhat troublesome. But, stranger, they never stick twice in the same place; and give them a fair chance for a few months, and you will get as much above noticing them as an alligator. They can't hurt my feelings, for they lay under the skin; and I never knew but one case of injury resulting from them, and that was to a Yankee: and they take worse to foreigners, any how, than they do to natives. But the way they used that fellow up! first they punched him until he swelled up and busted; then he su-per-a-ted, as the doctor called it, until he was as raw as beef; then he took the ager, owing to the warm weather, and finally he took a steamboat and left the country. He was the only man that ever took mosquitoes to heart that I know of. But mosquitoes is natur, and I never find fault with her. If they ar large, Arkansaw is large, her varmints ar large, her trees ar large, her rivers ar large, and a small mosquito would be of no more use in Arkansaw than preaching in a cane-brake."

This knock-down argument in favour of big mosquitoes used the Hoosier up, and the logician started on a new track, to explain how numerous bear were in his "diggins," where he represented them to be "about as plenty as blackberries, and a little plentifuler."

Upon the utterance of this assertion, a timid little man near me inquired if the bear in Arkansaw ever attacked the settlers in numbers.

"No," said our hero, warming with the subject, "no, stranger, for you see it ain't the natur of bar to go in droves; but the way they squander about in pairs and single ones is edifying. And then the way I hunt them the old black rascals know the crack of my gun as well as they know a pig's squealing. They grow thin in our parts, it frightens them so, and they do take the noise dreadfully, poor things. That gun of mine is perfect *epidemic among bar;* if not watched closely, it will go off as quick on a warm scent as my dog Bowie-knife will; and then that dog—whew! why the fellow thinks that the world is full of bar, he finds them so easy. It's lucky he don't talk as well as think; for with his natural modesty, if he should suddenly learn how much he is acknowledged to be ahead of all other dogs in the universe, he would be astonished to death in two minutes. Strangers, the dog knows a bar's way as well as a horse-jockey knows a woman's: he always barks at the right time, bites at the exact place, and whips without getting a scratch. I never could tell whether he was made expressly to hunt bar, or whether bar was made expressly for him to hunt: any way, I believe they were ordained to go together as naturally as Squire Jones says a man and woman is, when he moralizes in marrying a couple. In fact, Jones once said, said he, 'Marriage according to law is a civil contract of divine origin; it's common to all countries as well as Arkansaw, and people take to it as naturally as Jim Dogget's Bowie-knife takes to bar.'"

"What season of the year do your hunts take place?" inquired a gentlemanly foreigner, who, from some peculiarities of his baggage, I suspected to be an Englishman, on some hunting expedition, probably at the foot of the Rocky Mountains.

"The season for bar hunting, stranger," said the man of Arkansaw, "is generally all the year round, and the hunts take place about as regular. I read in history that varmints have their fat season, and their lean season. That is not the case in Arkansaw, feeding as they do upon the *spontenacious* productions of the sile, they have one continued fat season the year round: though in winter things in this way is rather more greasy than in summer, I must admit. For that reason bar with us run in warm weather, but in winter, they only waddle. Fat, fat! it's an enemy to speed; it tames everything that has plenty of it. I have seen wild turkeys, from its influence, as gentle as chickens. Run a bar in this fat condition, and the way it improves the critter for eating is amazing; it sort of mixes the ile up with meat, until you can't tell t'other from which. I've done this often. I recollect one perty morning in particular, of putting an old fellow on the stretch, and considering the weight he carried, he run well. But the dogs soon tired him down, and when I came up with him wasn't he in a beautiful sweat—I might say fever; and then to see his tongue sticking out of his mouth a feet, and his sides sinking and opening like a bellows, and his cheeks so fat he couldn't look cross. In this fix I blazed at him, and pitch me naked into a briar patch if the steam didn't come out of the bullet-hole ten foot in a straight line. The fellow, I reckon, was made on the high-pressure system, and the lead sort of bust his biler."

"That column of steam was rather curious, or else the bear must have been *warm*," observed the foreigner, with a laugh.

"Stranger, as you observe, that bar was WARM, and the blowing off of the steam show'd it, and also how hard the varmint had been run. I have no doubt if he had kept on two miles farther his insides would have been stewed; and I expect to meet with a varmint yet of extra bottom, who will run himself into a skinfull of bar's grease: it is possible, much onlikelier things have happened."

"Whereabouts are these bears so abundant?" inquired the foreigner, with increasing interest.

"Why, stranger, they inhabit the neighbourhood of my settlement, one of the prettiest places on old Mississippi—a perfect location, and no mistake; a place that had some defects until the river made the 'cut-off' at 'Shirt-tail bend,' and that remedied the evil, as it brought my cabin on the edge of the river—a great advantage in wet weather, I assure you, as you can now roll a barrel of whiskey into my yard in high water from a boat, as easy as falling off a log. It's a great improvement, as toting it by land in a jug, as I used to do, *evaporated* it too fast, and it became expensive. Just stop with me, stranger, a month or two, or a year if you like, and you will appreciate my place. I can give you plenty to eat; for beside hog and hominy, you can have bar-ham, and bar-sausages, and a mattress of bar-skins to sleep on, and a wildcat-skin, pulled off hull, stuffed with corn-shucks, for a pillow. That bed would put you to sleep if you had the rheumatics in every joint in your body. I cal that ar bed a *quietus.* Then look at my land—the government ain' got another such a piece to dispose of. Such timber, and such bottom land, why you can't preserve any thing natural you plant in it unless you pick it young, things thar will grow out of shape so quick. I once planted in those diggins a few potatoes and beets: they took a fine start, and after that an ox team couldn't have kept them from growing. About that time I went off to old Kentuck on bisiness, and did not hear from them things in three months, when I accidentally stumbled on a fellow who had stopped at my place, with an idea of buying me out. 'How did you like things?' said I. 'Pretty well,' said he; 'the cabin is convenient, and the timber land is good; but that bottom land ain't worth the first red cent.' 'Why?' said I. ' 'Cause,' said he. ' 'Cause what?' said I. ' 'Cause it's full of cedar stumps and Indian mounds,' said he, *'and it can't be cleared.'* 'Lord,' said I, 'them ar "cedar stumps" is beets, and them ar "Indian mounds" ar tater hills.' As I expected, the crop was overgrown and useless: the sile is too rich, *and planting in Arkansaw is dangerous.* I had a good-sized sow killed in that same bottom land. The old thief stole an ear of corn, and took it down where she slept at night to eat. Well, she left a grain or two on the ground, and lay down on them: before morning the corn shot up, and the percussion killed her dead. I don't plant any more: natur intended Arkansaw for a hunting ground, and I go according to natur."

The questioner who thus elicited the description of our hero's settlement, seemed to be perfectly satisfied, and said no more; but the "Big Bar of Arkansaw" rambled on from one thing to another with a volubility perfectly astonishing, occasionally disputing with those around him, particularly with a "live Sucker" from Illinois, who had the daring to say that our Arkansaw friend's stories "smelt rather tall."

In this manner the evening was spent; but conscious that my own association with so singular a personage would probably end before morning, I asked him if he would not give me a description of some particular bear hunt; adding that I took great interest in such things, though I was no sportsman. The desire seemed to please him, and he squared himself round towards me, saying, that he could give me an idea of a bar hunt that was never beat in this world, or in any other. His manner was so singular, that half of his story consisted in his excellent way of telling it, the great peculiarity of which was, the happy manner he had of emphasizing the prominent parts of his conversation.

As near as I can recollect, I have italicized them, and given the story in his own words.

"Stranger," said he, "in bar hunts *I am numerous,* and which particular one, as you say, I shall tell, puzzles me. There was the old she devil I shot at the Hurricane last fall—then there was the old hog thief I popped over at the Bloody Crossing, and then—Yes, I have it! I will give you an idea of a hunt, in which the greatest bar was killed that ever lived, *none excepted;* about an old fellow that I hunted, more or less, for two or three years; and if that ain't a particular bar hunt, I ain't got any to tell. But in the first place, stranger, let me say, I am pleased with you because you ain't ashamed to gain information by asking, and listening and that's what I say to Countess's pups every day when I'm home; and I have got great hopes of them ar pups, because they are continually *nosing* about; and though they stick it sometimes in the wrong place, they gain experience any how, and may learn something useful to boot. Well, as I was saying about this big bar, you see when I and some more first settled in our region, we were drivin to hunting naturally; we soon liked it, and after that we found it an easy matter to make the thing our business. One old chap who had pioneered 'afore us, gave us to understand that we had settled in the right place. He dwelt upon its merits until it was affecting, and showed us, to prove his assertions, more marks on the sassafras trees than I ever saw on a tavern door 'lection time. 'Who keeps that ar reckoning?' said I. 'The bar,' said he. 'What for?' said I. 'Can't tell,' said he; 'but so it is: the bar bite the bark and wood too, at the highest point from the ground they can reach, and you can tell, by the marks,' said he, 'the length of the bar to an inch.' 'Enough,' said I. 'I've learned something here a'ready, and I'll put it in practice.'

"Well, stranger, just one month from that time I killed a bar, and told its exact length before I measured it, by those very marks; and when I did that, I swelled up considerable—I've been a prouder man ever since. So I went on, larning something every day, until I was reckoned a buster and allowed to be decidedly the best bar hunter in my district; and that is a reputation as much harder to earn than to be reckoned first man in Congress, as an iron ramrod is harder than a toadstool. Did the varmint grow over-cunning by being fooled with by green-horn hunters, and by this means get troublesome, they send for me as a matter of course; and thus I do my own hunting, and most of my neighbours'. I walk into the varmints though, and it has become about as much the same to me as drinking. It is told in two sentences—a bar is started, and he is killed. The thing is somewhat monotonous now—I know just how much they will run, where they will tire, how much they will growl, and what a thundering time I will have in getting them home. I could give you the history of the chase with all particulars at the commencement, I know the signs so well—*Stranger, I'm certain.* Once I met with a match though, and I will tell you about it; for a common hunt would not be worth relating.

"On a fine fall day, long time ago, I was trailing about for bar, and what should I see but fresh marks on the sassafras trees, about eight inches above any in the forests that I knew of. Says I, 'them marks is a hoax, or it indicates the d——t bar that was ever grown.' In fact, stranger, I couldn't believe it was real, and I went on. Again I saw the same marks, at the same height, and *I knew the thing lived.* That conviction came home to my soul like an earthquake. Says I, 'here is something a-purpose for me: that bar is mine, or I give up the hunting business.' The very next morning what should I see but a number of buzzards hovering over my cornfield. 'The rascal has been there,' said I, 'for that sign is certain:' and, sure enough, on examining, I found the bones of what had been as beautiful a hog the day before, as was ever raised by a Buckeye. Then I tracked the critter out of the field to the woods, and all the marks he left behind, showed me that he was *the bar.*

"Well, stranger, the first fair chase I ever had with that big critter, I saw him no less than three distinct times at a distance: the dogs run him over eighteen miles and broke down, my horse gave out, and I was as nearly used up as a man can be, made on *my* principle, *which is patent.* Before this adventure, such things were unknown to me as possible; but, strange as it was, that bar got me used to it before I was done with him; for he got so at last, that he would leave me on a long chase *quite easy.* How he did it, I never could understand. That a bar runs at all, is puzzling; but how this one could tire down and bust up a pack of hounds and a horse, that were used to overhauling everything they started after in no time, was past my understanding. Well, stranger, that bar finally go so sassy, that he used to help himself to a hog off my premises whenever he wanted one; the buzzards followed after what he left, and so between *bar and buzzard,* I rather think I was *out of pork.*

"Well, missing that bar so often took hold of my vitals, and I wasted away. The thing had been carried to far, and it reduced me in flesh faster than an ager. I would see that bar in every thing I did: *he hunted me,* and that, too, like a devil, which I began to think he was. While in this fix, I made preparations to give him a last brush, and be done with it. Having completed every thing to my satisfaction, I started at sunrise, and to my great joy, I discovered from the way the dogs run, that they were near him; finding his trail was nothing, for that had become as plain to the pack as a turnpike road. On we went, and coming to an open country, what should I see but the bar very leisurely ascending a hill, and the dogs close at his heels, either a match for him in speed, or else he did not care to get out of their way—I don't know which. But wasn't he a beauty, though? I loved him like a brother.

"On he went, until he came to a tree, the limbs of which formed a crotch about six feet from the ground. Into this crotch he got and seated himself, the dogs yelling all around it; and there he sat eyeing them as quiet as a pond in low water. A green-horn friend of mine, in company, reached shooting distance before me, and blazed away, hitting the critter in the centre of his forehead. The bar shook his head as the ball struck it, and then walked down from that tree as gently as a lady would from a carriage. 'Twas a beautiful sight to see him do that—he was in such a rage that he seemed to be as little afraid of the dogs as if they had been sucking pigs; and the dogs warn't slow in making a ring around him at a respectful distance, I tell you; even Bowie-knife, himself, stood off. Then the way his eyes flashed—why the fire of them would have singed a cat's hair; in fact that bar was in a *wrath all over.* Only one pup came near him, and he was brushed out so totally with the bar's left paw, that he entirely disappeared; and that made the old dogs more cautious still. In the mean time, I came up, and taking deliberate aim as a man should do, at his side, just back of his foreleg, *if my gun did not snap,* call me a coward, and I won't take it personal. Yes, stranger, *it snapped,* and I could not find a cap about my person. While in this predicament, I turned round to my fool friend—says I, 'Bill,' says I, 'you're an ass—you're a fool—you might as well have tried to kill that bar by barking the tree under his belly, as to have done it by hitting him in the head. Your shot has made a tiger of him, and blast me, if a dog gets killed or wounded when they come to blows, I will stick my knife into your liver, I will—' my wrath was up. I had lost my caps, my gun had snapped, the fellow with me had fired at the bar's head, and I expected every moment to see him close in with the dogs, and kill a dozen of them at least. In this thing I was mistaken, for the bar leaped over the ring formed by the dogs, and giving a fierce growl, was off—the pack, of course, in full cry after him. The run this time was short, for coming to the edge of a lake the varmint jumped in, and swam to a little island in the lake, which it reached just a moment before the dogs. 'I'll have him now,' said I, for I had found my caps in the *lining of my coat*—so, rolling a log into the lake, I paddled myself across to the island, just as the dogs had cornered the bar in a thicket. I rushed up and fired—at the same time the critter leaped over the dogs and came within three feet of me, running like mad; he jumped into the lake, and tried to mount the log I had just deserted, but every time he got half his body on it, it would roll over and send him under; the dogs, too, got around him, and pulled him about, and finally Bowie-knife clenched with him, and they sunk into the lake together. Stranger, about this time, I was excited, and I stripped off my coat, drew my knife, and intended to have taken a part with Bowie-knife myself, when the bar rose to the surface. But the varmint staid under—Bowie-knife came up alone, more dead than alive, and with the pack came ashore. 'Thank God,' said I, 'the old villain has got his deserts at last.' Determined to have the body, I cut a grape-vine for a rope, and dove down where I could see the bar in the water, fastened my queer rope to his leg, and fished him, with great difficulty, ashore. Stranger, may I be chawed to death by young alligators, if the thing I looked at wasn't a *she bar, and not the old critter after all.* The way matters got mixed on that island was onaccountably curious, and thinking of it made me more than ever convinced that I was hunting the devil himself. I went home that night and took to my bed—the thing was killing me. The entire team of Arkansaw in bar-hunting, acknowledged himself used up, and the fact sunk into my feelings like a snagged boat will in the Mississippi. I grew as cross as a bar with two cubs and a sore tail. The thing got out 'mong my neighbours, and I was asked how come on that individu-al that never lost a bar when once started? and if that same individu-al didn't wear telescopes when he turned a she bar, of ordinary size, into an old he one, a little larger than a horse? 'Perhaps,' said I, 'friends'—getting wrathy—'perhaps you want to call somebody a liar,' 'Oh, no,' said they, 'we only heard such things as being *rather common* of late, but we don't believe one word of it; oh, no,'—and then they would ride off and laugh like so many hyenas over a dead man. It was too much, and I determined to catch that bar, go to Texas, or die,—and I made my preparations accordin'. I had the pack shut up and rested. I took my rifle to pieces and iled it. I put caps in every pocket about my person, *for fear of the lining.* I then told my neighbours, that on Monday morning—naming the day—I would start THAT BAR, and bring him home with me, or they might divide my settlement among them, the owner having disappeared. Well, stranger, on the morning previous to the great day of my hunting expedition, I went into the woods near my house, taking my gun and Bowie-knife along, just *from habit,* and there sitting down also from habit, what should I see, getting over my fence, but *the bar*! Yes, the old varmint was within a hundred yards of me, and the way he walked *over that fence*—stranger, he loomed up like a *black mist,* he seemed so large, and he walked right towards me. I raised myself, took deliberate aim, and fired. Instantly the varmint wheeled, gave a yell, and *walked through the fence* like a falling tree would through a cobweb. I started after, but was tripped up by my inexpressibles, which either from habit, or the excitement of the moment, were about my heels, and before I had really gathered myself up, I heard the old varmint groaning in a thicket near by, like a thousand sinners, and by the time I reached him he was a corpse. Stranger, it took five men and myself to put the carcase on a mule's back, and old long-ears waddled under the load, as if he was foundered in every leg of his body, and with a common whopper of a bar, he would have trotted off, and enjoyed himself. 'Twould astonish you to know how big he was: I made a *bed-spread of his skin,* and the way it used to cover my bar mattress, and leave several feet on each side to tuck up, would have delighted you. It was in fact a creation bar, and if it had lived in Samson's time, and had met him, in a fair fight, it would have licked him in the twinkling of a dice-box. But, strangers, I never like the way I hunted, and *missed him.* There is something curious about it, I could never understand,—and I never was satisfied at his giving in so easy at last. Perhaps, he had heard of my preparations to hunt him the next day, so he jist come in, like Capt. Scott's coon, to save his wind to grunt with in dying; but that ain't likely. My private opinion is, that that bar was an *unhuntable bar, and died when his time come.*"

When the story was ended, our hero sat some minutes with his auditors in a grave silence; I saw there was a mystery to him connected with the bear whose death he had just related, that had evidently made a strong impression on his mind. It was also evident that there was some superstitious awe connected with the affair,—a feeling common with all "children of the wood," when they meet with any thing out of their everyday experience. He was the first one, however, to break the silence, and jumping up, he asked all present to "liquor" before going to bed,—a thing which he did, with a number of companions, evidently to his heart's content.

Long before day, I was put ashore at my place of destination, and I can only follow with the reader, in imagination, our Arkansas friend, in his adventures at the "Forks of Cypress" on the Mississippi.

# Pecos Bill Discovers He Is a Human

## James Cloyd Bowman

NOT long after Grandy's disappearance, a remarkable adventure befell Cropear. He was, at the time, hunting across the rolling mesa. He had just stopped to examine a stretch of grassy plain where the prairie dogs had built themselves a city. The prairie dogs were making merry as if playing at hide-and-seek in and out of their hidden doorways.

Cropear was lying on the ground stretched out on his stomach and resting on his elbows, his chin in his palms. He suddenly became aware of the dull *tlot, tlot* of an approaching broncho. This was not strange, for he had often met ponies. But now he became conscious of a strange odor. Cropear prided himself on knowing every scent of every animal in his part of the world. This, however, was different; it tickled his nose and was like fire in the wild grasses. It was, in fact, the first whiff of tobacco he had smelled since he was a child, and it awakened in him a vague memory of a world of long lost dreams.

Immediately Cropear became curious and forgot for the moment the first and most universal law of the Pack—the law of staying put, of sitting so still that he could not be seen. He sat up suddenly and threw his head about to see what this strange smell might be. There, but a few yards distant, the buckskin cow pony and his rider, Chuck, came to a sudden, slithering halt.

Cropear suddenly let out three scared yelps and turned on his heels to run away. Chuck—himself a perfect mimic—repeated the scared yelps. This aroused Cropear's curiosity further. He stopped and let out another series of yelps. These Chuck again repeated. In the Coyote language, Cropear was asking, "Who are you? Who are you?" Chuck was repeating this question without in the least knowing what the yips meant.

Thus began the most amusing dialogue in all the history of talk. Cropear would bark a question over and over, and in reply Chuck would mimic him perfectly.

Cropear kept galloping in circles, curiously sniffing, and wondering when and where it was he had smelled man and tobacco.

Chuck kept his hand on his gun and his eyes on the strange wild creature. He couldn't help admiring the sheer physical beauty of this perfect, healthy wild man. Every muscle was so fully developed that he looked like another Hercules.

Cropear was, in fact, as straight as a wagon-tongue. His skin, from living all his life in the open sunlight and wind, was a lustrous brown, covered with a fine silken fell of burnished red hair. Over his shoulders lay the bristling mane of his unshorn locks.

After an hour or two of galloping about, Cropear lost much of his fear, approached nearer, and squatted down on his haunches to see what would happen.

"You're a funny baby!" Chuck laughed.

"Funny baby," Cropear lisped like a child of four.

The cowpuncher talked in a low, musical accent; and slowly and brokenly at first, Cropear began to prattle. He was taking up the thread of his speech where he had dropped it years before when he was lost by his family.

For nearly a month Chuck wandered around on the mesa and continued his dialogue with Cropear. Chuck would patiently repeat words and sentences many times. He was forced to use his hands and arms and his face and voice to illustrate all that he said. But Cropear proved such an apt pupil that soon he was saying and understanding everything. What's more, Cropear's speech became far more grammatical than Chuck's own, for only the finest language had ever been permitted among the Coyotes. And Cropear had evolved a combination of the two. The worst he ever said from then on, in cowboy lingo, was just an ain't or two.

Chuck was astonished at the speed with which he learned. "He's brighter'n a new minted dollar!" Chuck declared to his broncho.

Over and over Chuck asked Cropear, "Who in the name of common sense are you, anyhow?" Cropear tried his best to remember, yet all he knew was that he was a Coyote. "But who are you?" Cropear asked in turn.

"My real name is Bob Hunt," Chuck laughed, "but the boys all call me Chuckwagon because I'm always hungry—Chuck for short." He drawled his words musically as he swung into an easy position across his saddle. "What are you doin', runnin' around here naked like a wild Coyote, that's what I want to know?"

"I *am* a Coyote," Cropear snapped back.

"Coyote, nothin'! You're a *human!*"

"An accursed *human!* I guess not! I wouldn't belong to that degraded *inhuman* race for anything in the world. Haven't I got fleas? Don't I hunt with the pack and run the fleet prong-horn Antelope and the spry Jack-rabbit off their legs? And don't I sit on my haunches, and don't I have my place in the circle, and don't I howl at night in accordance with the ancient approved custom of all thoroughbred Coyotes? Don't you suppose I know who I am as well as you?" Cropear answered quite out of patience.

"You've just been eatin' of the locoweed and are a little out of your head," laughed Chuck. "Besides, every human in Texas has got fleas, so that's got nothin' at all to do with it."

"I haven't been eating of the locoweed! Only silly cattle and mustangs do a thing like that. I *am* in my right mind—and what's more, I *am* a Coyote!"

"You're loco, or else I am," insisted the smiling Chuck. "Why, you're a *human* just the same as I am. Don't you know that every Coyote's got a long bushy tail? Now, you ain't got no tail at all and you know it."

Strange as it may seem, this was the first time that Cropear had really looked himself over, and sure enough, he saw at once that he had no tail.

"But no one has ever before said that to me. Perhaps—no, I won't believe it. I don't want to be a depraved *inhuman*. . . . I know, for all you say, that I'm a full-blooded noble Coyote!"

Because of his sudden fears, Cropear was fighting to hold to his belief.

"If you wasn't so perfectly serious about it all, you'd be a downright scream," Chuck cackled. "As it is, I almost pity you."

"You're the one who needs to be pitied," snarled Cropear. "Anyone that's got to be an *inhuman* needs pity. Here you sit with a piece of cowhide over your head, the wool of the sheep over your shoulders and legs, and calfskin over your feet. Why, you can't even use your own legs. You've got to have a broncho to carry you around fast. Me, an *inhuman* human, no!" Cropear fairly spat his words, he was so disgusted.

*"Human!"* Chuck continued. *"Human!* Why, say, you're the only perfect human critter I've ever laid eyes on. If I had the muscles you've got, I'd turn in some mornin' before breakfast and beat up every prize fighter in all creation, and that within an inch of his life."

"But you haven't yet proved I'm not a noble Coyote," Cropear added with stubborn courage.

"It's proof you want, is it? Well, then, come with me and I'll give you all the proof you'll ever need, and that in a hurry."

Chuck swung his idle foot into the stirrup, spun his pony around like a top, and struck out in the direction of the Pecos River. At first he walked his broncho, but Cropear trotting along in front of him, set a faster stride. Next he paced his pony, but still Cropear ran far ahead and beckoned him to follow. Soon he was galloping at full tilt. The broncho was doing its best, but Cropear idled along at a graceful lope that seemed easier than walking. Chuck rubbed his eyes and could not believe that Cropear could run so far and so fast.

When they arrived at the river, Chuck led Cropear down to the water's edge. Here he found a quiet pool beside the racing current, where the reflection made a perfect mirror.

"Wade in a bit. There, stand still, lean over and look at yourself," Chuck commanded.

While Cropear was leaning over the water without an idea in the world that he was looking at himself, Chuck began to kick off his clothes. "Look at what you see down below there," he called. "Ain't we as alike as two mustangs from the same herd?"

Cropear obeyed. There, in the water, he saw a creature who looked like Chuck—but didn't. What was it? Cropear moved his head to the left, and the creature's head moved in the same direction. He moved to the right. The creature moved the other way.

Was Chuck right, then? It was an appalling thought. That he was an *inhuman,* after all, was so terrible to Cropear, he was without words for reply. For a long moment, he stood silent and motionless. Then he looked down at his reflection again. Surely this was all a bad dream!

Now Chuck waded in and threw his arm around the sorrowful boy's shoulder. "Come on down," he said, pulling Cropear in beside him. "Now look. Here I am and there you are."

Without a doubt, there was Chuck's reflection. And there, beside him, must be Cropear, the coyote. An *inhuman!* Nothing could possibly be worse.

Just at this instant, Chuck caught sight of a strange mark on Cropear's upper right arm—a tattooed star, showing plainly through the red fell of hair.

"I'll be locoed if I ain't got one of them, too," he cried, pointing to a similar mark on his own arm.

Cropear looked first at his arm, then at Chuck's. "What does it mean?" he asked, slowly.

"It means you're found. You're my little lost brother Bill. You ain't Cropear and you ain't never been."

Cropear stood stone still. "Your brother?"

"Surest thing you know. Listen. This is how I know. When Dad was travelin' around once with a Patent Medicine Man, he learned how to do this here tattooin'. So when us kids arrived, Mother got the idea it'd be a good thing to have a big star on the arm of each and every one of us. She said she didn't intend any of us ever to forget the Lone Star State we belonged to. And what's more, if any one of us happened to get lost, this star would help find us. So, as usual, Mother was right! You got lost but you're found again. See?"

"Now you sound as if you're the one that's been eating of the locoweed and gone crazy," Cropear replied.

"It's the honest truth, I'm tellin' you. I'd be willin' to stand on a stack of Bibles as high as the moon and repeat every word of it out in public, if you'd but quit your foolish notion that you're a varmint."

"Varmint, indeed!" Cropear snarled. "You're completely locoed. It's the pale-faced *inhumans* that are low-down varmints! Coyotes are the noblest of all the earth's creatures!"

Fortunately Chuck was so interested in the story he was just beginning that he did not take time to answer this last insult.

"Honestly, Cropear—Bill, I mean. This is what happened. Our family was goin' along from the Brazos River valley down to the Rio Grande. Dad was drivin' a little east Texas spotted cow and a little wall-eyed spavined roan horse. They was hitched to an old covered wagon with wooden wheels made from cross sections of a sycamore tree. Mother'd insisted it was gettin' too crowded up there in Texas, and she wanted to be where there was at least elbow room."

"Your mother must have had a wide sweep of elbows," Cropear commented.

"Yes, we lived a hundred miles from the nearest town and seventy-five miles from the nearest tradin' post. But an immigrant settled down thirty-five miles away, and Mother said we'd got to move. She couldn't have any stranger settlin' in her back yard, she said."

"What kind of woman was she, anyway?" Cropear asked curiously.

"Well, judge for yourself. She swept forty-five Indian Chiefs out of her back yard with her broomstick one mornin' before breakfast. You see, she found them prowlin' around, set on doin' mischief, and she sent them flyin' with one swoop and never give it more never mind than as if they was a bunch of sage chickens, or meddlesome porcupines.

"You probably don't remember it, but you cut your teeth on a Bowie knife that Davy Crockett sent our mother as a present when he heard what a brave, wise woman she was."

"Well, that's the kind of mother I have always dreamed I would like. Perhaps I am partly *human,* after all," Cropear now conceded. This mother sounded very fine indeed!

"Well, as we was migratin' in the covered wagon," Chuck continued without noticing the remark, "I guess you jumped overboard right along about here. Half a day passed before the rest of us discovered that you was missin', and then when we come back, we couldn't find you."

"My mother must have loved me dearly!" Cropear snarled, bitterly resentful that he could have meant as little to so splendid a person. "Not missing me for half a day! Nothing like that ever happened between me and Grandy. Why, he loved me so he never allowed me out of his sight for a single minute, day or night!"

"You don't get the idea at all," Chuck continued. "You see, it was like this. You had eighteen brothers and sisters, more or less. Well, after you was lost overboard, there was still seventeen of us flounderin' around in the covered wagon. One more or less didn't make no difference. Besides, there was one younger than you was—Henrietta—and she was mewlin' and droolin' in your dear mother's arms up on the front seat beside your father, the whole of the way. Your older sister, Sophrina, was supposed to look after you, but she got to quarrelin' with brother Hoke. He was teasin' her about her best beau, that had been left behind on the Brazos, at the edge of our thirty-five-mile back yard. So it was perfectly natural for you to jump overboard when no one was lookin', and then not be missed for a long time."

"So that was it," Cropear said as in a dream. "But when my mother discovered that I was gone, what then?"

"Well, it was the old story of the 'Ninety and Nine' all over again each day, ever after. Your mother had the whole seventeen of us to feed and look after; but she was often talkin' about her Little Lost Bill. Sometimes she put in the Pecos part, for the last sight she had of you was when she inspected things just before the wagon started to ford this river. She used to wake up in the middle of the night and get to thinkin' the Coyotes and Grizzly

Bears was crunchin' your tender bones. And I can hear her yet, at table, sighin' as she looked at your vacant chair. Her last words when she died were, 'Now I'll be seein' Little Bill!'"

"The dear good woman," Cropear sighed, in genuine relief, "but I can never love her as I love Grandy. And what about my father?"

Chuck laughed loud and long. "He was a regular copperas breeches and one gallus kind of man. He had seven dogs, a cob pipe and a roll of home-spun tobacco stuck down his pocket. He would spend more time pokin' a rabbit out of a hollow tree than he would to secure shelter for his family in a storm. He could easily afford to have one or two of his children blow away, but rabbits was too scarce to take the chance of losin' one! You see, he didn't count for much with Mother. A woman who could sweep out forty-five big Indian Chiefs with a single broom-handle couldn't be expected to show much mercy for a mere husband.

"Besides, she'd never have been able to scare the Big Chiefs so easily if she hadn't been practisin' up on her own old man! Fact is, she was the cock of the walk at our ranch. Dad merely took orders. We nicknamed him Moses. But Mother was the God of the Mountain! She wrote her commands on tables of stone and the poor man who received them from her hands was meek. I'm tellin' you, he was meek!"

"Your story begins to sound reasonable, and I do agree that I now see a faint likeness between us. . . . But I don't want to be an *inhuman!* I don't want to have to wear clothes and ride horses. I want to be free! I want to continue to be strong. I want to be healthy like my brothers, the Bears, the Wolves, and the Coyotes, who are wild and natural and vigorous! I want to live where I can lay me down on a sheet of mist and roll up in a blanket of fog. I want to sleep where I can breathe the clean air and see the countless eyes of all my brother animals peeping down at me as they race across the sky!"

"Don't be a fool, brother. It's high time for you to forget that you was ever called Cropear. It's right and proper for you now to become Pecos Bill. Come with me and I'll take you to the ranch house, where you'll be happier than you've ever been yet."

"But I can't think of going with you today. I've at least got to go back and take my farewell of the Pack."

"Well then, tomorrow. Tomorrow I'll come for you. And I'll say we'll teach you the gentlest of all ancient arts, the art of the ranch. Oh yes, you'll still be right in the great out-of-doors. With your strength like an ox and your spry heels, you'll become the greatest of all the great cowmen the world has ever known."

Chuck's words stirred something deep within Cropear's nature. What it was, he did not know. But he saw clearly in this instant, that come what might, he must go with Chuck. Lifting his head with a gesture of determination, he said solemnly, "Brother Chuck, I hear the call! Today I bid you adieu; tomorrow I join you!"

With these words and without once looking back, Cropear loped easily over the chappiro, across the rolling mesa. He skirted the sage brush and was soon lost in the haze of the distant mesquite.

Chuck rubbed his eyes for a moment to make certain that this was something more than a day dream. Then he pulled on his high-heeled boots, tightened his jingling spurs, swung aboard his astonished buckskin pony and was off. All the way home to the ranch house he sang so loud that he fairly cracked his voice:

"With my seat in the sky and my knees in the saddle,
I'm going to teach Pecos Bill to punch Texas cattle.
   Get along, little dogies, get along, get along;
   Get along, little dogies, get along.
   Coma ti yi youpy, youpy ya!
   Coma ti yi youpy, youpy ya!"

# He

## Katherine Anne Porter

LIFE was very hard for the Whipples. It was hard to feed all the hungry mouths, it was hard to keep the children in flannels during the winter, short as it was: "God knows what would become of us if we lived north," they would say: keeping them decently clean was hard. "It looks like our luck won't never let up on us," said Mr. Whipple, but Mrs. Whipple was all for taking what was sent and calling it good, anyhow when the neighbors were in earshot. "Don't ever let a soul hear us complain," she kept saying to her husband. She couldn't stand to be pitied. "No, not if it comes to it that we have to live in a wagon and pick cotton around the country," she said, "nobody's going to get a chance to look down on us."

Mrs. Whipple loved her second son, the simple-minded one, better than she loved the other two children put together. She was forever saying so, and when she talked with certain of her neighbors, she would even throw in her husband and her mother for good measure.

"You needn't keep on saying it around," said Mr. Whipple, "you'll make people think nobody else has any feelings about Him but you."

"It's natural for a mother," Mrs. Whipple would remind him. "You know yourself it's more natural for a mother to be that way. People don't expect so much of fathers, some way."

This didn't keep the neighbors from talking plainly among themselves. "A Lord's pure mercy if He should die," they said. "It's the sins of the fathers," they agreed among themselves. "There's bad blood and bad doings somewhere, you can bet on that." This behind the Whipples' backs. To their faces everybody said, "He's not so bad off. He'll be all right yet. Look how He grows!"

Mrs. Whipple hated to talk about it, she tried to keep her mind off it, but every time anybody set foot in the house, the subject always came up, and she had to talk about Him first, before she could get on to anything else. It seemed to ease her mind. "I wouldn't have anything happen to Him for all the world, but it just looks like I can't keep Him out of mischief. He's so strong and active, He's always into everything; He was like that since He could walk. It's actually funny sometimes, the way He can do anything; it's laughable to see Him up to His tricks. Emly has more accidents; I'm forever tying up her bruises, and Adna can't fall a foot without cracking a bone. But He can do anything and not get a scratch. The preacher said such a nice thing once when he was here. He said, and I'll remember it to my dying day, 'The innocent walk with God—that's why He don't get hurt.'" Whenever Mrs. Whipple repeated these words, she always felt a warm pool spread in her breast, and the tears would fill her eyes, and then she could talk about something else.

He did grow and He never got hurt. A plank blew off the chicken house and struck Him on the head and He never seemed to know it. He had learned a few words, and after this He forgot them. He didn't whine for food as the other children did, but waited until it was given Him; He ate squatting in the corner, smacking and mumbling. Rolls of fat covered Him like an overcoat, and He could carry twice as much wood and water as Adna. Emly had a cold in the head most of the time—"she takes that after me," said Mrs. Whipple—so in bad weather they gave her the extra blanket off His cot. He never seemed to mind the cold.

Just the same, Mrs. Whipple's life was a torment for fear something might happen to Him. He climbed the peach trees much better than Adna and went skittering along the branches like a monkey, just a regular monkey. "Oh, Mrs. Whipple, you hadn't ought to let Him do that. He'll lose His balance sometime. He can't rightly know what He's doing."

Mrs. Whipple almost screamed out at the neighbor. "He *does* know what He's doing! He's as able as any other child! Come down out of there, you!" When He finally reached the ground she could hardly keep her hands off Him for acting like that before people, a grin all over His face and her worried sick about Him all the time.

"It's the neighbors," said Mrs. Whipple to her husband. "Oh, I do mortally wish they would keep out of our business. I can't afford to let Him do anything for fear they'll come nosing around about it. Look at the bees, now. Adna can't handle them, they sting him up so; I haven't got time to do everything, and now I don't dare let Him. But if He gets a sting He don't really mind."

"It's just because He ain't got sense enough to be scared of anything," said Mr. Whipple.

"You ought to be ashamed of yourself," said Mrs. Whipple, "talking that way about your own child. Who's to take up for

Him if we don't, I'd like to know? He sees a lot that goes on, He listens to things all the time. And anything I tell Him to do He does it. Don't never let anybody hear you say such things. They'd think you favored the other children over Him."

"Well, now I don't, and you know it, and what's the use of getting all worked up about it? You always think the worst of everything. Just let Him alone, He'll get along somehow. He gets plenty to eat and wear, don't He?" Mr. Whipple suddenly felt tired out. "Anyhow, it can't be helped now."

Mrs. Whipple felt tired too, she complained in a tired voice. "What's done can't never be undone, I know that as good as anybody; but He's my child, and I'm not going to have people say anything. I get sick of people coming around saying things all the time."

In the early fall Mrs. Whipple got a letter from her brother saying he and his wife and two children were coming over for a little visit next Sunday week. "Put the big pot in the little one," he wrote at the end. Mrs. Whipple read this part out loud twice, she was so pleased. Her brother was a great one for saying funny things. "We'll just show him that's no joke," she said, "we'll just butcher one of the sucking pigs."

"It's a waste and I don't hold with waste the way we are now," said Mr. Whipple. "That pig'll be worth money by Christmas."

"It's a shame and a pity we can't have a decent meal's vittles once in a while when my own family comes to see us," said Mrs. Whipple. "I'd hate for his wife to go back and say there wasn't a thing in the house to eat. My God, it's better than buying up a great chance of meat in town. There's where you'd spend the money!"

"All right, do it yourself then," said Mr. Whipple. "No wonder we can't get ahead!"

The question was how to get the little pig away from his ma, a great fighter, worse than a Jersey cow. Adna wouldn't try it: "That sow'd rip my insides out all over the pen." "All right, old fraidy," said Mrs. Whipple, *"He's* not scared. Watch *Him* do it." And she laughed as though it was all a good joke and gave Him a little push towards the pen. He sneaked up and snatched the pig right away from the teat and galloped back and was over the fence with the sow raging at His heels. The little black squirming thing was screeching like a baby in a tantrum, stiffening its back and stretching its mouth to the ears. Mrs. Whipple took the pig with her face stiff and sliced its throat with one stroke.

When He saw the blood He gave a great jolting breath and ran away. "But He'll forget and eat plenty, just the same," thought Mrs. Whipple. Whenever she was thinking, her lips moved making words. "He'd eat it all if I didn't stop Him. He'd eat up every mouthful from the other two if I'd let Him."

She felt badly about it. He was ten years old now and a third again as large as Adna, who was going on fourteen. "It's a shame, a shame," she kept saying under her breath, "and Adna with so much brains!"

She kept on feeling badly about all sorts of things. In the first place it was the man's work to butcher; the sight of the pig scraped pink and naked made her sick. He was too fat and soft and pitiful-looking. It was simply a shame the way things had to happen. By the time she had finished it up, she almost wished her brother would stay at home.

Early Sunday morning Mrs. Whipple dropped everything to get Him all cleaned up. In an hour He was dirty again, with crawling under fences after a possum, and straddling along the rafters of the barn looking for eggs in the hayloft. "My Lord, look at you now after all my trying! And here's Adna and Emly staying so quiet. I get tired trying to keep you decent. Get off that shirt and put on another, people will say I don't half dress you!" And she boxed Him on the ears, hard. He blinked and blinked and rubbed His head, and His face hurt Mrs. Whipple's feelings. Her knees began to tremble, she had to sit down while she buttoned His shirt. "I'm just all gone before the day starts."

The brother came with his plump healthy wife and two great roaring hungry boys. They had a grand dinner, with the pig roasted to a crackling in the middle of the table, full of dressing, a pickled peach in his mouth and plenty of gravy for the sweet potatoes.

"This looks like prosperity all right," said the brother; "you're going to have to roll me home like I was a barrel when I'm done."

Everybody laughed out loud; it was fine to hear them laughing all at once around the table. Mrs. Whipple felt warm and good about it. "Oh, we've got six more of these; I say it's as little as we can do when you come to see us so seldom."

He wouldn't come into the dining room, and Mrs. Whipple passed it off very well. "He's timider than my other two," she said, "He'll just have to get used to you. There isn't everybody He'll make up with, you know how it is with some children, even cousins." Nobody said anything out of the way.

"Just like my Alfy here," said the brother's wife. "I sometimes got to lick him to make him shake hands with his own grand-mammy."

So that was over, and Mrs. Whipple loaded up a big plate for Him first, before everybody. "I always say He ain't to be slighted, no matter who else goes without," she said, and carried it to Him herself.

"He can chin Himself on the top of the door," said Emly, helping along.

"That's fine. He's getting along fine," said the brother.

They went away after supper. Mrs. Whipple rounded up the dishes, and sent the children to bed and sat down and unlaced her shoes. "You see?" she said to Mr. Whipple. "That's the way my whole family is. Nice and considerate about everything. No out-of-the-way remarks—they *have* got refinement. I get awfully sick of people's remarks. Wasn't that pig good?"

Mr. Whipple said, "Yes, we're out three hundred pounds of pork, that's all. It's easy to be polite when you come to eat. Who knows what they had in their minds all along?"

"Yes, that's like you," said Mrs. Whipple. "I don't expect anything else from you. You'll be telling me next that my own brother will be saying around that we made Him eat in the kitchen! Oh, my God!" She rocked her head in her hands, a hard pain started in the very middle of her forehead. "Now it's all spoiled, and everything was so nice and easy. All right, you don't like them and you never did—all right, they'll not come here again soon, never you mind! But they *can't* say He wasn't dressed every lick as good as Adna—oh, honest, sometimes I wish I was dead!"

"I wish you'd let up," said Mr. Whipple. "It's bad enough as it is."

It was a hard winter. It seemed to Mrs. Whipple that they hadn't ever known anything but hard times, and now to cap it all a winter like this. The crops were about half of what they had a right to expect; after the cotton was in it didn't do much more than cover the grocery bill. They swapped off one of the plow horses, and got cheated, for the new one died of the heaves. Mrs. Whipple kept thinking all the time it was terrible to have a man you couldn't depend on not to get cheated. They cut down on everything, but Mrs. Whipple kept saying there are things you can't cut down on, and they cost money. It took a lot of warm clothes for Adna and Emly, who walked four miles to school during the three-months session. "He sets around the fire a lot, He won't need so much," said Mr. Whipple. "That's so," said Mrs. Whipple, "and when He does the outdoor chores He can wear your tarpaullion coat. I can't do no better, that's all."

In February He was taken sick, and lay curled up under His blanket looking very blue in the face and acting as if He would choke. Mr. and Mrs. Whipple did everything they could for him for two days, and then they were scared and sent for the doctor. The doctor told them they must keep Him warm and give Him plenty of milk and eggs. "He isn't as stout as He looks, I'm afraid," said the doctor. "You've got to watch them when they're like that. You must put more cover onto Him, too."

"I just took off His big blanket to wash," said Mrs. Whipple ashamed. "I can't stand dirt."

"Well, you'd better put it back on the minute it's dry," said the doctor, "or He'll have pneumonia."

Mr. and Mrs. Whipple took a blanket off their own bed and put His cot in by the fire. "They can't say we didn't do everything for Him," she said, "even to sleeping cold ourselves on His account."

When the winter broke He seemed to be well again, but He walked as if His feet hurt Him. He was able to run a cotton planter during the season.

"I got it all fixed up with Jim Ferguson about breeding the cow next time," said Mr. Whipple. "I'll pasture the bull this summer and give Jim some fodder in the fall. That's better than paying out money when you haven't got it."

"I hope you didn't say such a thing before Jim Ferguson," said Mrs. Whipple. "You oughtn't to let him know we're so down as all that."

"That ain't saying we're down. A man is got to look ahead sometimes. He can lead the bull over today. I need Adna on the place."

At first Mrs. Whipple felt easy in her mind about sending Him for the bull. Adna was too jumpy and couldn't be trusted. You've got to be steady around animals. After He was gone she started thinking, and after a while she could hardly bear it any longer. She stood in the lane and watched for Him. It was nearly three miles to go and a hot day, but He oughtn't to be so long about it. She shaded her eyes and stared until colored bubbles floated in her eyeballs. It was just like everything else in life, she must always worry and never know a moment's peace about anything. After a long time she saw Him turn into the side lane, limping. He came on very slowly, leading the big hulk of an animal by a ring in the nose, twirling a little stick in His hand, never looking back or sideways, but coming on like a sleepwalker with His eyes half shut.

Mrs. Whipple was scared sick of bulls; she had heard awful stories about how they followed on quietly enough, and then suddenly pitched on with a bellow and pawed and gored a body to pieces. Any second now that black monster would come down on Him, my God, He'd never have sense enough to run.

She mustn't make a sound nor a move; she mustn't get the bull started. The bull heaved his head aside and horned the air at a fly. Her voice burst out of her in a shriek, and she screamed at Him to come on, for God's sake. He didn't seem to hear her clamor, but kept on twirling His switch and limping on, and the bull lumbered along behind him as gently as a calf. Mrs. Whipple stopped calling and ran towards the house, praying under her breath: "Lord, don't let anything happen to Him. Lord, you *know* people will say we oughtn't to have sent Him. You *know* they'll say we didn't take care of Him. Oh, get Him home, safe home, safe home, and I'll look out for Him better! Amen."

She watched from the window while He led the beast in, and tied him up in the barn. It was no use trying to keep up, Mrs. Whipple couldn't bear another thing. She sat down and rocked and cried with her apron over her head.

From year to year the Whipples were growing poorer and poorer. The place just seemed to run down of itself, no matter how hard they worked. "We're losing our hold," said Mrs. Whipple. "Why can't we do like other people and watch for our best chances? They'll be calling us poor white trash next."

"When I get to be sixteen I'm going to leave," said Adna. "I'm going to get a job in Powell's grocery store. There's money in that. No more farm for me."

"I'm going to be a schoolteacher," said Emly. "But I've got to finish the eighth grade, anyhow. Then I can live in town. I don't see any chances here."

"Emly takes after my family," said Mrs. Whipple. "Ambitious every last one of them, and they don't take second place for anybody."

When fall came Emly got a chance to wait on table in the railroad eating-house in the town near by, and it seemed such a shame not to take it when the wages were good and she could get her food too, that Mrs. Whipple decided to let her take it, and not bother with school until the next session. "You've got plenty of time," she said. "You're young and smart as a whip."

With Adna gone too, Mr. Whipple tried to run the farm with just Him to help. He seemed to get along fine, doing His work and part of Adna's without noticing it. They did well enough until Christmas time, when one morning He slipped on the ice coming up from the barn. Instead of getting up He thrashed round and round, and when Mr. Whipple got to Him, He was having some sort of fit.

They brought Him inside and tried to make Him sit up, but He blubbered and rolled, so they put Him to bed and Mr. Whipple rode to town for the doctor. All the way there and back he worried about where the money was to come from: it sure did look like he had about all the troubles he could carry.

From then on He stayed in bed. His legs swelled up double their size, and the fits kept coming back. After four months, the doctor said, "It's no use, I think you'd better put Him in the County Home for treatment right away. I'll see about it for you. He'll have good care there and be off your hands."

"We don't begrudge Him any care, and I won't let Him out of my sight," said Mrs. Whipple. "I won't have it said I sent my sick child off among strangers."

"I know how you feel," said the doctor. "You can't tell me anything about that, Mrs. Whipple. I've got a boy of my own. But you'd better listen to me. I can't do anything more for Him, that's the truth."

Mr. and Mrs. Whipple talked it over a long time that night after they went to bed. "It's just charity," said Mrs. Whipple, "that's what we've come to, charity! I certainly never looked for this."

"We pay taxes to help support the place just like everybody else," said Mr. Whipple, "and I don't call that taking charity. I think it would be fine to have Him where He'd get the best of everything . . . and besides, I can't keep up with these doctor bills any longer."

"Maybe that's why the doctor wants us to send Him—he's scared he won't get his money," said Mrs. Whipple.

"Don't talk like that," said Mr. Whipple, feeling pretty sick, "or we won't be able to send Him."

"Oh, but we won't keep Him there long," said Mrs. Whipple. "Soon's He's better, we'll bring Him right back home."

"The doctor has told you and told you time and again He can't ever get better, and you might as well stop talking," said Mr. Whipple.

"Doctors don't know everything," said Mrs. Whipple, feeling almost happy. But anyhow in the summer Emly can come home for a vacation, and Adna can get down for Sundays: we'll all work together and get on our feet again, and the children will feel they've got a place to come to."

All at once she saw it full summer again, with the garden going fine, and new white roller shades up all over the house, and Adna and Emly home, so full of life, all of them happy together. Oh, it could happen, things would ease up on them.

They didn't talk before Him much, but they never knew just how much He understood. Finally the doctor set the day and a neighbor who owned a double-seated carryall offered to drive them over. The hospital would have sent an ambulance, but Mrs. Whipple couldn't stand to see Him going away looking so sick as all that. They wrapped Him in blankets, and the neighbor and Mr. Whipple lifted Him into the back seat of the carryall beside Mrs. Whipple, who had on her black shirt waist. She couldn't stand to go looking like charity.

"You'll be all right, I guess I'll stay behind," said Mr. Whipple. "It don't look like everybody ought to leave the place at once."

"Besides, it ain't as if He was going to stay forever," said Mrs. Whipple to the neighbor. "This is only for a little while."

They started away, Mrs. Whipple holding to the edges of the blankets to keep Him from sagging sideways. He sat there blinking and blinking. He worked His hands out and began rubbing His nose with His knuckles, and then with the end of the blanket. Mrs. Whipple couldn't believe what she saw; He was scrubbing away big tears that rolled out of the corners of His eyes. He sniveled and made a gulping noise. Mrs. Whipple kept saying, "Oh, honey, you don't feel so bad, do you? You don't feel so bad, do you?" for He seemed to be accusing her of something. Maybe He remembered that time she boxed His ears, maybe He had been scared that day with the bull, maybe He had slept cold and couldn't tell her about it; maybe He knew they were sending Him away for good and all because they were too poor to keep Him. Whatever it was, Mrs. Whipple couldn't bear to think of it. She began to cry, frightfully, and wrapped her arms tight around Him. His head rolled on her shoulder: she had loved Him as much as she possibly could, there were Adna and Emly who had to be thought of too, there was nothing she could do to make up to Him for His life. Oh, what a mortal pity He was ever born.

They came in sight of the hospital, with the neighbor driving very fast, not daring to look behind him.

# How I Won the War

## Robert Flynn

THE whole world was at war and everyone had to sacrifice. That's what the movie stars, and even President Roosevelt, said. Dad was in the Pacific. Mother ran the service station and came home dirty every night and so tired she had to rest before fixing supper. "Everyone has to help if we're going to win the war," she said. I walked home after school; we lived on forty acres outside of town. I fed the chickens, hogs and the milk cow, tended the victory garden, swept the floors and washed the dishes. Mother gave me fifty cents a week and I saved the money for a Victory Bond to buy bullets to help Dad fight the war.

Every Friday the teachers sold stamps that you could glue in a little book until you had enough for a Victory Bond. Mother gave me money for a stamp every week in addition to my allowance. Billy Crutchfield bragged that he bought two stamps every week. His dad was the banker, and the government wouldn't let him fight in the war because women couldn't run the bank, Billy said. Harold Tedford bragged about the scrap metal he collected from his dad's farms. He sold it and used the money to go to the picture show every Friday night with Billy Crutchfield and some of the other kids.

Mother said I could use my allowance to go to the picture show if I wanted to, and I did sometimes if it was something special like *Wake Island*, but mostly I saved the money to buy a bond. I was going to save my allowance until I had enough, and when the teacher asked who wanted to buy a stamp I was going to say, "I want to buy a bond." I could imagine the look on Billy's face. Harold's too, and a lot of the other kids.

Harold's brother was a mechanic at an airfield in Kansas and sent Harold wings made of some metal alloy. Harold wore them like his brother was a pilot. Billy's dad was given a collar pin like soldiers wore for leading a bond drive at the bank and Billy wore it to school sometimes. Dad didn't send me any souvenirs; he didn't even write many letters. Mother said there weren't any stores in the Pacific, but I knew it was because he was too busy fighting. I wanted my dad home more than anything and I had saved fifteen dollars when a man came down the road leading a horse.

Not many people came by on horseback anymore, just farmers and ranchers trying to save gas and tires.

I saw them when the horse fell. The man kicked and beat the horse until it got up. He rode a little ways and the horse fell again. The third time it fell, he beat and kicked the horse until it got back on its feet, but it almost fell again when he tried to get back in the saddle. After that the man led the horse until it fell in front of the house. He yelled at the horse, pulled on the reins and kicked it. The horse got halfway to its feet then fell.

I walked out to the road. The man was small and dried up and maybe too old to be in the army. His clothes were dirty and he had an old blanket tied to his saddle. "What's the matter with your horse?" I asked. Its sides were heaving, its neck was lathered and it was blowing bloody foam out of its nostrils.

"Just lazy. You folks couldn't give me a ride into town could you?"

"Nobody here but me," I said.

The man nodded. He studied the horse. "I ain't never going to get to town like this. Sorry sack of . . . bones." He kicked the horse again.

"Is he your horse?" I asked, surprised that anyone would kick his own horse.

"He is until I can sell him for dog food. If I can get him to town." He gave me a sidelong glance. "You don't think your folks might want to buy a horse, do you?"

I wanted a horse more than anything except winning the war and seeing Dad again. "Would you be willing to sell him to me?"

He studied me, not directly but looking at me sideways from under his hat that was torn and too big for his head. "How much you got to buy him with?"

"I got fifteen dollars but I'm saving that to buy a Vict—"

"You just bought yourself a horse."

I was stunned, not just that he accepted but by the speed of it. Nobody bought anything without dickering for a while.

"You ain't going to go back on your word, are you?" he asked.

Dad thought that going back on your word was about the lowest thing a man could do, except maybe being a slacker or hoarding things that were rationed. I wasn't sure how he felt about someone saving money to buy a bond to win the war and then buying a horse for himself with it. "I've been saving to buy a Victory Bond," I said.

"You can't buy no bond for fifteen dollars. Now, if you had a horse, rested him a few days, you could sell him for enough to buy a bond, maybe two bonds."

"Really?" I kneeled in the road and stroked the horse. Its muzzle was hot. Its eyes bulged. "What's his name?"

"This horse? Why, this is . . . Blaze. See that white on his forehead. That's called a blaze. That's how he got his name."

"How you doing, Blaze?" I asked, rubbing behind his ears. The horse eyed me indifferently. For fifteen dollars I could buy a real horse, a horse of my own. Wouldn't Mother be surprised? She might be disappointed that I didn't buy a bond, but when I explained that I could sell Blaze for two bonds—Blaze nudged me and I hugged his lathered neck. I knew I couldn't sell Blaze, not even for two bonds.

"I wouldn't sell him except that, well, in Fort Worth they make airplanes to fight the war. I want to help make them planes and I can't take the horse with me. That's why I'm willing to let you have him for fifteen dollars. That is some bargain, boy. Patriotic too."

I thought of me and Blaze riding up in the schoolyard and all the kids watching. Then I thought of Dad in the Pacific. "I don't know," I said.

"Get back and I'll get the son of a . . . I'll get him up so you can look at him," the man said, ready to kick Blaze some more.

"No. Don't."

"I want you to see the kind of horse you're getting."

"He's fine. I just planned to buy a Victory Bond."

"Well, I got to get him up and get on the road then. I don't want to hold up them airplanes just because he's tired."

I didn't want to hold up the war effort either; I just couldn't make up my mind to let my dream come true when everybody else was sacrificing to win the war.

"You know anything about horses, son?"

"No sir," I admitted, although I feared he was going to tell me I didn't know enough to buy a horse.

"This here is a thoroughbred, the finest horse in the world."

I could buy Blaze for fifteen dollars, let him rest for a couple of days and give him to the army, and maybe after the war was over and Dad and Blaze came home, they'd give him back. After they didn't need him anymore. I thought of Blaze leading a charge, or maybe dragging a cannon up at just the right time.

"Can a thoroughbred pull a heavy load?"

"You let old Blaze rest a couple of days and he can pull any wagon you got."

I didn't have a wagon but Harold Tedford's father did. Maybe he would loan me the wagon and I could hitch Blaze to it and pick up scrap metal. And I'd use that money to buy a bond. I could take the horse to school and during recess give kids a ride for a nickel, and when the teacher asked who wanted to buy a stamp, I'd pour the money out on her desk and tell her I wanted as many as I could buy. For a moment I saw President Roosevelt appearing at a school assembly and calling me and Blaze up on the stage to thank us for the bonds we had bought. Or the army might give me a collar pin like they gave Billy's dad.

"Get back, kid. I got to get the horse up and get going."

"Wait," I said. "I'll get the money." I ran to the house and when I got back he was kicking Blaze again. "What are you doing?"

"I didn't sell the saddle and bridle," he said. He had already pulled off the bridle and he hit Blaze with the reins.

I said, "Don't hit him anymore. I'll help you get the saddle."

We tugged and pulled and he kicked at the horse until we got the saddle. With the bridle in his hand, he started down the road dragging the saddle. I sat beside Blaze and put my arms around his lathered neck. "He won't hurt you anymore," I said, as glad as Blaze was that the man had gone. "You rest a while and when you feel better I'll put you in the lot."

Blaze avoided looking me in the eye. I went to the barn, got a tub and started pulling grass for the horse. While I pulled grass, I thought of how we'd look riding to school. "He's a thoroughbred," I'd say. "Finest horse in the world." I'd give kids rides when they bought Victory stamps, and I'd collect scrap metal, and if they needed me to I could ride Blaze around town looking for spies and saboteurs.

I heard a car honking, saw a cloud of dust coming down the road and remembered Blaze lying in the middle of it. I ran to the road waving and yelling, "Stop." The car skidded into the bar ditch. "Get that horse out of the road before someone runs over it," the driver yelled. He stopped to pick up the man with the saddle, and I knew then that he would get to Fort Worth and that I had done the right thing to buy Blaze.

I also knew I was going to have to get Blaze out of the road. I caught hold of his mane but I couldn't move him. I got a rope from the barn and put it around his neck, but I still couldn't budge Blaze. I got the tub of grass and tried to coax him but Blaze ignored it. I sat down in the road, ready to cry. "You're going to get run over," I said. "Then I can't ride you or collect scrap or anything."

I went to the barn, filled a bucket with water and carried it to him. Blaze stuck his nose in the bucket and turned it over. I filled it again but he wouldn't drink it. I dipped water out of the bucket and washed the blood off his muzzle. I went to the house, got the slip off my pillow, and sat down beside Blaze, ready to wave down any car that came down the road. The first car was Mother.

"Jimmy, what are you doing in the road?"

"I can't get Blaze to move," I said. "Someone is going to run over him."

"Whose horse is it?"

"He's mine," I said, afraid my mother would think buying a horse instead of a bond wasn't the right thing to do. My chin was trembling and I couldn't make it stop. "I bought him with the money I was saving to buy a bond and now I can't get him out of the road and he's going to get run over."

Mother parked the car in front of the house and walked back to the road. She sat down and put her arm around me. She smelled like gasoline. "Tell me what happened," she said.

Between sniffs and nose wipes I told her about Blaze falling because he was tired, and the man beating him, and buying Blaze to buy bonds, and the car coming and Blaze not eating, and now I didn't know what to do.

"He was a bad man. He sold you an old horse that is dying."

"No. He's a thoroughbred, the finest kind of horse. He's just tired." I ducked my head so she wouldn't see any tears.

She hugged me closer and kissed the top of my head the way she did sometimes. "See all that gray on his face," she said. "He's an old horse and he's been mistreated and overworked. I don't think he's going to live." I knew she didn't think Blaze was a thoroughbred either. "You go in the house. I'll go get Mr. Tedford."

"Will he make Blaze feel better?"

"I think he'll want to put him out of his misery. We don't want him to suffer anymore, do we?" She put her hand on Blaze's head.

"Could we get the horse doctor? To be sure he's not just tired."

"He could be anywhere in the county, and with gas rationing —" Her voice trailed off. "I guess we ought to give your horse a chance."

"He said when Blaze got rested he would be worth two bonds. If he can get well I can sell rides on him. I can use him to collect scrap. I'll use the money to buy bonds."

"I'll get the vet but don't get your hopes up about the horse getting better. Go on to the house now. Don't you have some chores?"

"Can I stay out here with him? So a car doesn't hit him?"

She sighed. "Okay. Go get the lantern and light it. I don't want you out here in the road after dark without a lantern. As soon as you hear a car you start waving that lantern. But not so fast that you blow the light out. Are you going to be scared here by yourself?"

"No, ma'am." It wasn't exactly a lie. I wouldn't be scared if Blaze got up so I could ride him away if something bad came along.

I sat close beside Blaze so I could touch him. I had always wanted a horse, and now I had one even if he was old and tired. It was a long time before Mother came back with the vet, and only one car came along. The driver said, "I hope your horse gets to feeling better." He knew it was my horse and he knew Blaze and I were doing the best we could.

I thought about the war, and if I was being a slacker because I gave my Victory Bond for a horse. I thought about Dad and how I would have to explain what I had done.

Blaze's head started nodding, like he was trying to go to sleep. Then he put his head down and stretched out his legs like he was pawing. Then he just stopped. I knew he was dead before the vet got there, but I didn't tell Mom or the vet. I just couldn't. The vet said I had done all I could for him and that he would send somebody out to get him. "Not too late," Mom said. He looked at me and nodded. I knew Mom wanted them to take Blaze away while I was in school.

Mom and I sat with Blaze for a while. Just sitting there, not saying anything. Then I said, "For a little while my dream came true."

"Even in wartime, a lot of dreams come true for a little while."

"You don't think I let Dad down?"

"I think your father would have done the same thing."

"Really?"

"It takes more than just bullets to win a war," she said.

I didn't tell the kids at school about Blaze because I was afraid they'd laugh at me. But when I told Dad, he said Mother was right.

# Salvador Late or Early

## Sandra Cisneros

SALVADOR with eyes the color of caterpillar, Salvador of the crooked hair and crooked teeth, Salvador whose name the teacher cannot remember, is a boy who is no one's friend, runs along somewhere in that vague direction where homes are the color of bad weather, lives behind a raw wood doorway, shakes the sleepy brothers awake, ties their shoes, combs their hair with water, feeds them milk and corn flakes from a tin cup in the dim dark of the morning.

Salvador, late or early, sooner or later arrives with the string of younger brothers ready. Helps his mama, who is busy with the business of the baby. Tugs the arms of Cecilio, Arturito, makes them hurry, because today, like yesterday, Arturito has dropped the cigar box of crayons, has let go the hundred little fingers of red, green, yellow, blue, and nub of black sticks that tumble and spill over and beyond the asphalt puddles until the crossing-guard lady holds back the blur of traffic for Salvador to collect them again.

Salvador inside that wrinkled shirt, inside the throat that must clear itself and apologize each time it speaks, inside that forty-pound body of boy with its geography of scars, its history of hurt, limbs stuffed with feathers and rags, in what part of the eyes, in what part of the heart, in that cage of the chest where something throbs with both fists and knows only what Salvador knows, inside that body too small to contain the hundred balloons of happiness, the single guitar of grief, is a boy like any other disappearing out the door, beside the schoolyard gate, where he has told his brothers they must wait. Collects the hands of Cecilio and Arturito, scuttles off dodging the many schoolyard colors, the elbows and wrists criss-crossing, the several shoes running. Grows small and smaller to the eye, dissolves into the bright horizon, flutters in the air before disappearing like a memory of kites.

# Picture of His Father's Face

## Tomás Rivera

*Translated by Rolando Hinojosa*

NOTHING to it; all the picture salesmen from San Antonio had to do was to sit and wait, like turkey buzzards, my Pa said, 'cause it was the same every year when the people came back home after some seven months on the migrant trail. There'd be money in their pockets, so, right behind them, the picture salesmen. Nothing to it.

And they brought sample cases of pictures, frames, and black and white and color proofs, too. Here's how they dressed: white shirt first of all, and a tie to go with it. Sure. Respectable, see? And that's why *la raza*, the people, would open their doors to them. I mean, a shirt and a tie represented honesty and respectability. Nothing to it. Easier than stealing, right? . . . and that's what I'm talking about here, see?

You know how people are, how we all of us are wanting our kids to get ahead and be somebody? Wear a white shirt. And a tie. Sure.

And there they came down those dusty streets, sample cases handy, and they were ready to work the town and the people . . .

Once (and I remember it well, too) I'd gone with Pa on a visit; a call to a compadre's house, when one of the sales types shows up. And he looked hesitant at first, kind of timid. Pa's compadre, Don Mateo, he asked the salesman to come on in, sit, make yourself at home.

"Afternoon (he said), you-all doing all right? We got something new to show you this year. Sí, señor."

"Oh, yeah? And what's that?"

"Let me explain what I'm talking about. You give us a photograph, a picture, right?, and what we do is to amplify it, we make it larger, and that's what amplify means. And then, after that, here's what we do: put that picture on wood. Yes. Sort of rounded off, see? What we call three dimensional."

"And what's the reason for that?"

"Realism. Makes the person come alive, you might say. It-a, it sort of jumps out at you, see? Three dimensional. Here, let me show you this one here . . . This is part of what we do. How about that, eh? Like he's alive, right? It sure looks it, don't it?"

"Yeah, that's pretty good. Hold on a minute, I'm going to show it to my wife . . . (Will you look at this? Isn't that something. Come over here, will you?) . . . You know, we were talking, the wife and me, thinking of sending off some snapshots this year, making them bigger. Enlarging them, right? Ah . . . but this ought to cost quite a bit, am I right?"

"Not as much as you'd think. The problem is *the process*, do you know what I mean by that?"

"Ah-hah. How much money we talking about here?"

"Well, not as much as you'd think, like I said. How does thirty dollars sound? But first-class, rounded off, see? Three dimensional . . ."

"Well, thirty dollars does sound kind of steep to me. I thought I heard you say it wouldn't go much more than the old ones. And this is on the installment plan, you say?"

"Well, if it was up to me . . . but it happens that we got us a new sales supervisor this year, and with him, it's cash; cash on the barrelhead, I'm afraid. You know how it is, but he's also right in a way, see? It's good, first class, quality workmanship. It'd make a great picture for that table, see? Realer than real. Rounded off, like this one here. Here, hold it yourself. Fine work, right? And we can do it in a month, too. Everything. But what we need from you is to tell us what color clothing, hair, and like that; and then, before you know it, the month's gone by, and you got yourselves the genuine article here. For a lifetime. And listen to this: we'll throw in the frame, too. Free, gratis. And it'll take a month. Tops. And I wish we could do business, but this new supervisor, he wants to get paid on the nail. And he pushes us, see?"

"Oh, I like the work, all right. But it's the money; it's kind-a high."

"I know what you mean. But you got to agree that that's what we call first class goods, substantial, see? . . . and that's what we're looking at here. You never seen work like this in your life, am I right? On wood? Like that?"

"No, I sure haven't, but . . . here, I'll ask the wife again . . . What do you think, eh?"

"It's nice. I like it. A lot. Look, why don't we try one? See how it comes out. We like it, we get some more. Let's start off with Chuy's picture. That's the only one we got of him, though, God rest him . . ."

"She's right. We took it right here before he left for Korea; and he died there. See? Here's the picture we're talking about. You, ah, you think you can do that rounding off with this one? Like you say? Like he looks alive, kind of?"

"Absolutely. We do a lot of servicemen, yes ma'am. You see, in this rounding that we do, they're better than photographs or snapshots. A whole lot. Now, all I need's the size, but you got to tell me that; the size you want. Oh, and that free frame I talked about, you want it in a square shape? Round, maybe? What d'you say? What should I write down here?"

(Don Mateo looked at his wife) "What d'you think? Can we order the one?"

"Well, I already told you what I think. I'd like to have my boy looking like that. Rounded off, in color."

"Okay, write it up like that, but like I said: that's the only picture we got of the boy. So, you got to take good care of it. He was supposed to send us one in uniform, all fitted out, see? And with the Mexican and the United States flags around him. You seen 'em, right? But we never got that picture. What happened was that as soon as he got to Korea, we then heard from the government. Missing in action, they said. Missing. So you best take good care a-that photo there."

"We'll take good care of it, yessir. You can count on it. The company knows you all are making a sacrifice here; oh, yes. We don't want you to worry none. And you just wait when you get it back, cleaned up and everything. What's it gonna be? We put on a navy-blue uniform on 'im?"

"Can you really do that? He's not even wearing a uniform on this one."

"Nothing to it. We just kind of fix it in; what we call an *inlay* job. You know about that? On the wood, see? Here, let me show you these over here . . . See this one here? Well, that boy there didn't have no uniform on when they took his picture. Our company was the one that put it on him. How about that, eh? Blue is it? Navy-blue?"

"Oh yeah, sure."

"And don't you worry none about your boy's picture, okay?"

"How long till we get those pictures, you think?"

"Can't be too long, right? But it takes time on account of *the process*. It's good work. And these people sure know what they're doing, too. You notice? The people in the samples looked alive, real."

"Oh, yeah, I know they do good work, no denying that. It's just that it's been over a month, or more."

"Yeah, but don't forget: how many towns between here and San Antonio? They must've gone through every one, see? It'll probably take 'em more'n a month on account of all the business they did."

"Yeah, that's got to be it, then. Sure."

And then, two weeks after that last exchange, something happened. There'd been some hard rains in the region, and some kids fooling around near the city dump, over by those big drain pipes there, well, that's where the kids found the photographs! Wet, and most beyond recognition, worn out, through and through, and full of holes some of them. But they were the snapshots and the pictures, all right. You could see they were; most of them were the same size, and you could still make out some of the faces on them, too.

Sold! They'd been taken in, and that sure didn't take long to sink in. Taken. Like babies. And Pa's compadre, Don Mateo, he got so mad, so mad, he just took off to San Antonio; went after that guy who'd conned them good, who'd taken their money, who'd taken his Chuy's last picture.

"Well, Compadre, I'll tell you what I did; how I went about it. First off, I stayed with Esteban. Every morning I'd go out with him, to that stall of his, where he sells vegetables; the San Antonio *mercado,* that open-air veg market. Worked with him, loading and unloading, helping out, you know. But I had me a plan, a hunch; a hope, maybe. And I just knew I was going to run across that big city con man, yeah.

"Anyway, every morning after helping Esteban set up that stand of his, I'd walk around some of the barrios there, by the market. Got to see a lot, see? But by now, it wasn't the money so much. That mad kind-of wore off. It was the wife's crying, see? And that'd been Chuy's one and only picture, and we'd told the guy, too. The only one we had of him, and the wife crying all the time. So it wasn't the money so much, now. Oh, we'd found them all there in the sewers, but that snapshot was ruined. Nothing left, see?"

"But in San Antonio, Compadre? How would anyone go about finding a guy like that?"

"I'll make it short, Compadre. He himself showed up at Esteban's stall one day. Just like that! Bought himself some vegetables, he did, right there. And I saw him face to face. He saw me too, but he made out like he didn't know me, know who I was. Never seen me before, see? Oh, I made him right away, and then you know what happened? Let me say this, Compadre, when you're angry, really angry, but I mean really angry now, you don't forget a face or anything. It all comes clear somehow.

"Well, I came up to him, grabbed him, yeah I did, and he went *white* on me, scared. You bet, he was. And I said: 'I want my boy's picture. And I want it rounded off, like you said. Three di—mension. You got that?"

"And then I told him I'd eat him up and spit him out if he didn't come through with that portrait of his. Hmph. He didn't know what to do, where to start. But he did it. From memory, you understand? But he did it."

"Yeah? Well how did he do that, Compadre?"

"Well, that's a mystery, but with fear working overtime, I guess you might say you can remember *anything*, everything. And there it was, three days later, and I didn't have to go after him this time. There he was at Esteban's stall, picture and everything. Well, there it is, see it? Right behind you. Good piece of work, right?"

"Tell you the truth, Compadre, I can't remember what young Chuy looked like anymore . . . But he, ah, he was beginning to look like you, wasn't he?"

"He sure was, Compadre. And you know what people say when they see the picture? They say the same thing. Yeah. That Chuy, had my boy lived, he'd look a lot like me, they say. And there's the picture, here, let me get it for you. I—dentical, eh, Compadre? Him and me, right?"

# The Flat of the Land

## Diana García

FROM the roof of her house, Amparo gauged the tilt of the old
water tower with the name "Pixley" faintly outlined on the side.
It was hard to say how long the tower would still be visible: another week or two, depending on the mud's flow. Not that a
missing tower would make any difference in a place where the
only off-ramp was at least five miles west and the combination
store and restaurant with its dusty lunch counter was on the
abandoned side of old Highway 99. Maybe the girl with the
blonde hair and freckles who worked at the store or the girl's
mother or grandmother would notice when Amparo stopped
coming in for an occasional skinny hamburger and greasy fries.

The first time the mud caught Amparo's attention, it looked
like a harmless bubble in the ground. It was an April morning,
and she'd been hanging the wash out to dry on the clothesline
behind her house. She had scarcely paid attention when the
mud burped at her, distracted at the time by the breeze whip-
ping the clothes on the line and thinking that the shadowy
clouds overhead might contain some rain.

That had been almost six months ago. Amparo turned and
studied the flat expanse to the east and the Sequoia foothills in
the distance. At the point where the mud had first appeared, the
bubble had grown to the size of a pond. Here the land sank into
itself and followed the outline of some long-ago river, a few scattered cottonwoods the only clues to its crumbled banks. From
this source, the mud had developed an easterly flow that skirted
the stand of cottonwoods. Amparo wondered why the mud had
left the trees untouched.

On the land next to hers, bulldozers had carved foundations
for a style of house popular forty years earlier. From her roof,
the excavations looked like archaeological digs. By the time Amparo moved here, no one was left who could tell her why the development had been abandoned. All that remained of the original site was the water tower and the water main to her house.
The only other trace of water was the mud; how else would the
mud keep rising and spreading the way it did?

When the dimple of mud turned into a smile and then a six-
inch wide crevice that threatened to swallow her clothesline,

Amparo began to sense a possible threat to her hideaway. Up until now, she had kept her brothers and parents at bay by giving them a Fresno post office box address. She visited them as often as twice a month so that they wouldn't press her for more information about where or how she was living. They seemed satisfied knowing she was living alone and that her disability income was more than adequate for all her needs. She never talked about her son or her former husband, so they assumed she had laid those memories to rest. That damn mud, though, might spoil everything. At first she talked to it.

"What do you think you're doing? You have no business out here in this weather. The sun will bake you before the summer is over and then you'll have done all this work for nothing." When the sun didn't bake the oozing crack to a dry, light finish, she started asking, "Why don't you go downhill?"—indicating a direction opposite her house—"It's much easier than going uphill." The crack widened, its banks thickening and hardening, creating an impenetrable barrier within a few days' exposure to the sun.

Amparo trained herself not to think about the spreading mud. She listened to the Mexican stations on the radio. At night, she'd lie in bed and pretend the coyotes were talking to her instead of to the foothills and the jack rabbits. She'd answer, "Yes, manzanita does make the best cover," and, "No, the easiest way to get yourself killed is to expose yourself." She rarely turned the lights on after dark, afraid someone might see the glow and learn she had discovered the house.

The house was no secret, really. A developer had built the two-story structure as a marketing device and then abandoned it as too expensive: adobe walls like those of a Pueblo ruin and energy supplied by an underground cable and a solar-powered generator. At one time, someone else must have lived here. Perhaps it had been a retired construction worker, some laborer or cement finisher destined to end his days sweeping dust from the compacted dirt floors and enjoying the cool feel of the dark tan walls, secure in the knowledge that no one would look for him here—no former wives or children with grandchildren to bother him.

Now it was Amparo's house. She washed her clothes in a wringer-washer like the one her mother had taught her to use when she was a little girl, like the one she had used when her son was born, the one in which she had washed his diapers. She admired, as if they were someone else's, the bookshelves carved into the sixteen-inch-thick walls of the living room and bedroom. When she felt the need for exercise, she'd run up and down the steps to the second floor loft and master bedroom, chanting "upstairs and downstairs and in my lady's chamber." And, of course, there was the six-inch plumbing throughout, wide enough to handle anything, even a pot of scorched beans.

Not that she ate much these days. She still enjoyed her plain Cream of Wheat for breakfast every morning—her *atole,* she called it. For lunch and light snacks she had learned to eat seasonally, buying all her produce at the roadside stands along old Highway 99. There were almonds and raisins year-round; strawberries, peaches, tomatoes, and peppers during the summer. By early May she was tired of apples and oranges but with June came early corn and sometimes a melon or two. Dinner was always corn tortillas, beans, and rice. She made a pot of beans and another of rice every Sunday. Sometimes she'd toss some bits of chicken or beef along with a handful of garbanzos, some chopped onion, and cilantro into the steaming rice. Her biggest craving was grease; once or twice a month she'd drive to Pixley for a hamburger and fries at the store's lunch counter.

The day the mud licked the left front tire of her old white Studebaker Lark station wagon, Amparo drove to the store for a "grease bomb"—that's what she called the hamburgers. It was the first official day of summer. By then, the mud-filled crevice was about twenty yards long, six inches wide, and about a foot-and-a-half deep. That day at the lunch counter she'd asked the young girl's mother, "Did they used to have a mud bath around here that you know of?"

"What do you mean, mud bath?" the woman had answered, poking a few loose strands of dark brown hair underneath one of the pink foam rollers on her head. At least the rollers worked better than the torn hair net the woman usually wore. "You mean the hot springs?"

Amparo checked her fries for stray hairs before she dipped them in ketchup. She knew about the dots on the map called Fountain Springs, California Hot Springs, and Miracle Springs. No water at any of them. "No, not water. Mud. Did they ever have mud baths over by the old water tower?" Amparo asked, trying not to sound too curious.

"No, no mud. This is a desert." The woman had a droning voice, like an old record player at slow speed. "The only water for mud would have to come from the creeks. We haven't had enough water for the creeks to run in almost ten years."

The woman's mother had interrupted, "The last time I saw the Chocolate River—that's the old riverbed over by your house—was when I was still a girl at home. That was about seventy years ago when the flash flood tore out the old road right after the war." Almost as an afterthought the old woman had added, "You know, a long time ago, when my grandmother's grandmother came here from Illinois, it was all tule marshland like Three Rivers."

That was when Amparo began parking her Studebaker on the side of the house away from the cottonwoods.

After the mud ate the clothesline and then the smallest manzanita bush, the one farthest from the house, Amparo consoled herself with the thought that at least the muddy flow didn't interfere with her sewer line. By the Fourth of July, when the crevice reached a foot wide and the dried banks on each side made a slick sidewalk cooler than the surrounding earth, she had made some allowances for its existence. That night, she lit sparklers in the starlight. She jumped and danced from bank to bank, playing a cheery game, a combination of hopscotch and jump rope, remembering incantatory lyrics from first grade.

*Mother, Mother, I am sick.*
*Call the doctor, quick, quick, quick.*
*In comes the doctor, in comes the nurse,*
*In comes the lady with the alligator purse.*
*Out goes the doctor, out goes the nurse,*
*Out goes the lady with the alligator purse.*

In the morning, the crevice was fifty yards long—Amparo estimated this from the thirty-foot foundations on each side of her lot—and anywhere from three to four feet deep, depending on where she pushed an old mop handle into the ground. Much more than four feet deep and Amparo wouldn't have anything long enough to measure the depth. As it was, when she pushed the mop handle into the section closest to the biggest manzanita bush, her fingers could touch the slowly rising mud.

It was such fine, clean mud—no worms or sharp rocks. "How would you like some roses, an old grandiflora, a wine- or cinnamon-scented bush? Would you like that? I could plant a row on each side of the front yard, use some of your mud for fertilizer. I bet you'd make good fertilizer?" This last a question. It was hard to say what the mud wanted.

On July 15, her forty-fifth birthday, Amparo washed her

bathtub and sprayed it with rosewater. When the sun was at its highest, she started dragging buckets of warm mud to the tub, climbing the stairs to the master bathroom, careful not to slosh too much onto the floor. Not that it mattered. Once the mud set, it was hard to tell where the original dirt floor ended and the new layer of mud began.

Amparo patted the mud to remove any air pockets, then took off all her clothes. She combed her long, still mostly black hair until it sparked with static electricity. Carefully she packed mud into her hair, arranged the entire mass into a turban on top of her head. Then she delicately dipped her right toes into the mud. Thick, lukewarm liquid squeezed between her toes. She lowered herself into the tub and let the mud ooze above her knees, her crotch, her belly button. Eyes closed, she finally sank to her chest and leaned her head against the back of the tub.

She thrilled to the sensation, like that of someone holding her without making contact. It was as if she had lost half her body weight. She felt an unnatural buoyancy, an inability to touch the very bottom of the tub. With smooth, even strokes, she massaged a thick layer of mud on her face and behind her ears.

She felt her skin tighten as the mud dried. When the mud grew cooler than her body, she pulled the plug and watched the mud make its way down the drain in small gulps. Then she padded downstairs, mud dribbling in small clumps wherever she stepped too hard.

Amparo sat outside in the late afternoon sun, her legs stretched in front of her, the heat baking her body mask to a glossy finish. She studied the effect in the hand mirror. As long as she kept her body perfectly still, she looked like an ancient statue. All the wrinkles were gone, the deep lines around her eyes and forehead, the cellulite. And her back pain was gone.

Amparo stretched from her waist to touch her toes. Where the mud started to crack, she carefully peeled it away, conscious of the adhesivelike grip that caused her skin to redden wherever there was too much hair. Her skin had the firm smoothness of a ripened peach fresh from the tree. The pores on her nose had disappeared and her hair shone in the sunlight. She remembered how Sammy, her ex-husband, used to tell her that the first time he spotted her running her old black German shepherd in the park, the sun made her black-brown hair look like a comet. "How perfectly you've caught me," she told the mud, its slick surface stamped with the lines of her body. That night she fed the mud her leftover beans and rice.

In early August she spotted a possible hairline crack just to the right of the main crevice. She brushed the line with a manzanita branch and it seemed to go away. It was hard to say. By late August, when the hairline crack had lengthened to form a thin leg to a V, she was sure. This leg was aimed at the opposite corner of her house, and like the first leg, it pointed in the same direction. "Ahh, you want the foothills," she whispered.

At first, the mud's flow was indiscernible unless she sat for several minutes, her eyes focused on a mark she'd scratch into the still-damp sides of the widening cracks. Another trick she used to measure the mud's movement was to make little paper boats from old Christmas wrapping paper and watch them gently float and bob on the barely moving surface. By early October the mud flow was obvious—a steady movement east despite the three-year drought.

When she first found the house three years ago, its biggest attraction had been the roof, the easy access along the molded staircase that climbed in profile up the east wall of her second-floor bedroom to the roof escape. Amparo had always thought she would like to live in a house with a hidden staircase to some underground study; now she knew that her real dream had always been of such a skylight escape. She enjoyed climbing the stairs in the morning, sliding the double-construction skylights open. She'd clamber over the lip of the stairs and eat her *atole* on the roof, watching the day take hold. It was as if the house had been designed just for her.

Now she made the roof her lookout post; the mud would need guidance. "Foothills to the east, say 15 miles, straight flat land, hardly any sage," she announced her first day on the job. She listened to the mud's distinctive sound. She could hear it humming and swallowing, no longer baffled by its inability to lay claim to the house. There were no windows or doors on the east side of the first floor of the house. The mud waited at the weep holes and joints, sensitive to the loosening of a corner as the house gave ground.

The coyotes' yips and cries grew more distinct. She counted how long it took their echoes to reach her, much as she would count the space between a thunderclap and a lightning flash. When they lurked too long she belittled them, smirking at their mangy coats, "Try a little mud in your fur. You'll kill a few fleas that way, I assure you," and "I once had a jacket with a red fox fur." She relented when they turned tail and skulked away. The next night she left a pile of freshly grilled chicken breasts seasoned with rosemary.

On the day of the harvest moon, Amparo drove to the Fruit
Patch produce stand and bought the last of the zucchini, now
over a foot long and four inches in diameter. She chose a pump-
kin the size of her head, as well as a garland of dried red New
Mexico chili pods and a selection of Indian corn tied with twine.

At sunset, Amparo climbed to the roof and arranged the offer-
ings on favorite plates. She poured a mixture of *atole* topped
with raisins and walnuts in a mixing bowl. When the moon was
full overhead, she placed the plates and bowl in a star-shaped
pattern, one for her head, the others for her hands and feet.
Then she lay on the roof enjoying the cool breeze overhead.

To the mud she tossed an inconsequential aside. "Isn't it nice
not to have to worry about cleaning and cooking and washing
and worrying about someone all the time?" When the mud with-
drew like a sulky child and refused to respond to her chatter,
she confessed, "Yes, I give you credit for going uphill away from
the riverbed. I never would have thought of that."

To the house she offered soothing counsel. "We'll ride it out
together, the two of us. You'll see. I'll take good care of you." The
mud hiccupped and poured a thick sheen over the lot. Amparo
imagined how the land might have looked as an inland sea.
"Just think of all that water." She felt the house shiver.

In Amparo's dreams that night, a stand of cottonwoods turned
into a grove of ancient trees. Where a clothesline once twirled like
a giant umbrella, clumps of tule rushes danced in the surge of a
waxing moon. In the distance, the flat roof of a house bobbed
above the flat of the land that stretched toward the foothills.

And as she slept, the mud came close and caressed the base
of the house. It told of the excitement of heat lightening cast on
the horizon on summer evenings; of the tenderness of misty
sighs heaved from a roiled earth on snow-swept mornings; of a
world best viewed from a height of 1500 feet.

In turn, the house recounted the thrill of water tumbling over
a bed of smooth-ground gravel; of air so cold in autumn that
spawning salmon gasped when they broke the surface.

House and mud lingered over shared secrets, reveling in this
moment of discovery. The house openly admired the reflection of
stars on the moist surface of the mud. In turn, the mud thrilled
to the crusted surface of the house, each trowel-stroke another
mystery to be explored.

In the predawn hours, Amparo awoke to the lurch of the house
lifting and settling on a wide river of mud. House and mud paused

as she clambered to the roof. They allowed her time to adjust her stance to the house's uncommon roll, then the house made a slow 180-degree turn from the old highway to the foothills.

Like a swimmer learning a new stroke, the house muscled through the mud, at first tentatively, then with increased fluidity. Loose pieces of masonry scattered as the house and mud picked up speed. The mud wash kicked up nearly one story high, flattening sage and manzanita.

"We're coming, we're coming, it won't be long before we're there," Amparo shouted to the hills. To the sun she complained, "We need some light over here. How do you expect us to see where we're going if you wait until six o'clock to get up?" To the house and mud she instructed, "Faster, go faster, we're almost there! Don't worry about me." As they drew closer, a cleft in the foothills parted, and house, mud, woman squeezed through in an eruption of closely contained forms, aiming for the tree-laced meadow above.

Through the temporary opening could be seen air so clear the sky looked like cut crystal, a passage so smooth that a traveler could press one hand against each side and never feel the moment of contact.

# The Snakeman

## Luci Tapahonso

THE child slid down silently and caught herself at the end of the fire escape. She eased herself down until she felt the cold, hard sidewalk through her slippers—then she let go.

The night was clear and quiet. The only noise that could be heard was the echo of the child's footsteps in the moonlit alley behind the old, brick buildings.

The little girls, watching her from the top floor of the dorm, swung the window screen in and out, catching it before it struck the window frame. They always talked about what would happen if the top hinges suddenly gave way but they hadn't yet.

"Good thing—it's spring," one of them said.

"She would freeze her toes off for sure," another hissed.

"SHHH-H," the biggest one hissed.

They whispered in lispy voices and someone on the other side of the room would only hear "s . . . sss," hissing and an occasional "shut-up!" The room was large with windows on three sides. The fire escape the child slid down was in the center of the north windows, which faced a big, dark hill, its slope covered with huge, round rocks and dry tumbleweeds. Opposite the fire escape was the door to the hall.

Sometimes the dorm mother, who lived at the other end of the hall, heard them giggling or running around. She would walk down the dark, shiny hall so fast her housecoat would fly behind her in billows. The girls would scurry to their beds, tripping over their long nightgowns, finally faking snores as she turned on the harsh, bright lights in each room. After she went back to her room, the children jumped up and laughed silently with wide, open mouths and pounded their fists into their beds.

One of the girls whispered loudly, "She's coming back." They all ran noiselessly to the window and watched the small figure coming. The little girl walked briskly with her hands in her housecoat pockets. She wore the soft, wool slippers all the little girls made for their sister or mother at Christmastime. But she had neither, so she wore them herself.

"Seems like she floats," one girl commented.

"How could she? Can't you hear her walking?" the biggest retorted.

The girls went back to their beds and the ones that were closest to the fire escape window opened the window and held it up until she was in. Then they all gathered at one bed and sat in the moonlight telling ghost stories or about how the end of the world was REALLY going to be. Except for the girl who left, she always went to sleep and wasn't noisy like the rest.

Sometimes late in the night or towards morning when the sun hadn't come up completely and everything was quiet and the room filled with the soft, even breathing of the children—one of them might stand at the window facing east and think of home far away and tears would stream down her face. Late in the night someone always cried and if the others heard her— they would pretend not to notice. They understood how it was with all of them . . . if only they could go to public school and eat at home everyday.

When they got up in the morning before they went downstairs to dress, two of them emptied their pockets of small, torn pieces of paper and scattered them under the beds. The beds had white ruffled bottoms that reached the floor and the bits of paper weren't visible unless one lifted the ruffles. This was the way they tested the girl that cleaned their room. When they returned to their bedroom in the evenings, they checked under their beds to see if the paper was gone. If it wasn't, they immediately reported it to the dorm mother, who never asked why they were so sure their room hadn't been cleaned.

The building was divided into three floors and an attic. The little girls who were in grade school occupied the bottom and top floors and the junior high girls had the middle floor. The top floor was used only for bedrooms and all daytime activity was on the bottom level. The building was old, like all the other buildings on campus, and the students were sure it was haunted. Besides, there was a graveyard a little ways away. How could it not be? they asked among themselves.

This was especially true for those little girls in the east end of the dorm, since they were so close to the attic door. There was a man in there, they always said in hushed voices, he always kept the attic door open just a little, enough to throw evil powder on anyone that walked by. For this reason, they all stayed out of the hallway at night. Once they had even heard him coming down the attic stairs to the door and the smaller girls started crying. They all slept two-to-a-bed, and the big girls made sure all the little girls had someone bigger with them. They stayed up

later than usual, crying and praying, so that no one woke early
enough to get everyone back into their right beds. The dorm
mother spanked each of them but at least, they said, that night
nothing happened to any of them.

Once when the little girl went on one of her walks at night,
the other children were waiting for her as they usually did. Two
of them were by the hall door trying to figure how to get to the
bathroom two doors down the hall when they heard a scratch-
ing noise outside on the sidewalk.

"You guys! come here! he's over here!!" they whispered loudly.

They ran to the east window and saw a dark figure go around
the corner and the biggest girl took control.

"You two get over by that window. You on that side. Someone
get on the fire escape in case he tries to get up here."

They watched the man below and tried to get a description of
him, in case someone asked them. They couldn't see him very
well because he was on the shady side of the building. Some of
the girls started crying, and some crawled quietly back into bed.
Two of them, the bigger ones, waited to open the window for the
other girl when she got back. When she came back, they all
huddled around her and told her and started crying again. She
said it was probably someone's father trying to see his daughter.
Probably the mother won't let him see her, she said. So the girls
calmed down and tried to figure out whose parents were di-
vorced or fought a lot. They finally decided that he was the
boyfriend of a junior high girl downstairs.

When a new girl came, she asked why the girl always walked
at night, and the biggest one had said:

"Wouldn't you if you could see your mother every night,
dummy?"

"Well, where's her mom? Can't she see her on weekends like
us? That's not fair."

"Fair? FAIR??" they had all yelled in disbelief.

Then the girl who walked explained that her parents had died
years before, when she was six, and they were buried at the
school cemetery. So that's why she went to see them. Just her
mother, mostly, though.

"How is she? Does she talk?"

"Can you REALLY see her?" the new girl asked.

"Yeah," she answered patiently. "She calls me and she waits
at the edge of the cemetery by those small, fat trees. She's real
pretty. When she died, they put a blue outfit on her. A Navajo

skirt that's real long and a shiny, soft, light blue blouse. She waves at me like this: 'Come here, shi yashil, my little baby.' She always calls me that. She's soft and smells so good."

The little girls all nodded, each remembering their own mothers.

"When it's cold or snowing, she lets me stand inside the blanket with her. We talk about when I was a baby, and what I'll do when I get big. She always worries if I'm being good or not."

"Mine, too," someone murmured.

"Why do mothers always want their girls to be goody-good?"

"So you won't die at the end of the world, dummy."

"Dying isn't *that* bad. You can still visit people like her mother does."

"But at the end of the world, all the dinosaurs and monsters that are sleeping in the mountains will bust out and eat the bad people. No one can escape, either," said the biggest girl with confidence.

Then the little girl who talked to her mother every night said quietly:

"No one can be that bad." She went to her bed and lay there looking at the ceiling until she fell asleep.

The other girls gathered on two beds and sat in a little circle and talked in tight, little voices about the snakeman who stole jewelry from some of the girls.

"You can't really see him," one said, "cause he's sort of like a blur, moves real fast and all you can see is a black thing go by."

"He has a silver bracelet that shines and if he shines it on you, you're a goner cause it paralyzes."

They talked about him until they began looking around to make sure he wasn't in the room.

The bigger girls slept with the littler ones, and they prayed that God wouldn't let that man in the attic or the snakeman come to them, and that the world wouldn't end until after their moms came to visit.

As the room got quiet and the breathing became even and soft, the little girl got up, put on her housecoat and slid soundlessly down the fire escape.

# Climbing the Mountain

## Julia M. Seton

IT was Commencement Day at a famous school, on the staff of which were several teachers of unique ideas.

The distribution of the awards, prizes, and symbols of progress, was put in the hands of a prominent individual who strongly disapproved of all such things, so that each child who received a token of success received also a sneering remark. For example, the boy who won first prize for regular attendance was told: "Here is your so-called prize. If you valued it as little as I do, you would throw it in the ash-can."

A little girl who came out first with her embroidery was told: "Here is the prize which I consider trash, and the purpose of it folly. The fact that you have done the thing should be your suffi-cient reward."

He cast a cloud on the whole affair. He humiliated children whose parents had come to rejoice in their success and tri-umph. Many were in tears over his remarks.

I was on the program to close the exercises with an Indian story. But I did not wait for my time to speak. As soon as this teacher ceased his sneering, I arose. I was boiling with indigna-tion, and said:

"I am down to tell you an Indian story at the finish of this session. I shall not wait till the finish. I will tell my story right now, and you can tie it to the distribution of these prizes."

And there and then, I fabricated the following story out of ele-ments which I had encountered before:

Afar in our dry Southwestern country is an Indian village, and in the offing is a high mountain towering up out of the desert. It was considered a great feat to climb this mountain, so that all the boys of the village were eager to attempt it.

One day, the Chief said: "Now, boys, you may all go to-day and try to climb the mountain. Start right after breakfast, and go each of you as far as you can. Then when you are tired, come back; but let each one bring me a twig from the place where he turned."

Away they went, full of hope, each feeling that he surely could reach the top.

Soon a fat, pudgy boy came slowly back, puffing and sweating. He stood before the Chief, and in his hand he held out a piece of cactus.

The Chief smiled and said: "My boy, you did not reach the foot of the mountain; you did not even get across the desert."

An hour later a second boy returned. He carried a twig of sagebrush.

"Well," said the Chief, "you reached the mountain's foot, but you did not even start the climb."

After another hour, a third boy came back. He held out a cottonwood spray.

"Good," said the Chief, "you got up as far as the springs."

A longer wait—and there came a boy with some buckthorn. The Chief smiled when he saw it, and spoke: "You were climbing. You were up to the first slide rock."

Later in the afternoon, one arrived with a cedar sprig, and the old man said: "Well done, my boy. You went half-way up."

An hour afterwards, one came with a branch of pine. To him the Chief said: "Good; you went to the third belt. You made three-quarters of the climb. Keep on trying. Next year you will undoubtedly reach the top."

The sun was low when the last returned. He was a tall, splendid boy of noble character; all knew he was marked for high emprise. He approached the Chief and held up his hand. It was empty. But his countenance was radiant as he spoke: "My father, there were no trees where I got to—I saw no twigs, no living thing upon the peak. But far and away I saw the shining sea."

Now the old man's face glowed, too, as he said aloud, and almost sang: "I knew it! I knew it when I looked upon your face. You have been to the top. It is written in your eyes and rings in your voice; it is vibrant in your frame. My boy, you need no twigs for token; you have felt the uplift, you have seen the glory of the mountain."

# Crok and the Crocodile

## Julia M. Seton

THE first word he said was "Mam mam," the second was "Goo goo"—which was quite the usual thing. But the third was "Crok crok." This was quite unusual, and it came months later. It was prompted by hearing a raven make similar sounds as it flew over—and that was why they named him "Crok."

This incident showed that Crok was an observer, as well as gifted with good control of his muscles. These things grew with him; so that, at the age of fifteen, Crok was a big, strong young hunter, well able to take care of himself in all the ordinary stress of life in the woods.

With the backward ken of history, I saw him standing on a ledge by the water—naked, brown, sinewy, strong, alert. This way and that he peered: every log in sight or partly hidden by the bushes, the water, or the bend of the bank, was keenly viewed and quickly comprehended. Not a line of bubbles in the stream but was seen and understood, for Crok had come to the ford, the crossing of the river, and he must pass. Although but fifteen years old, his father had sent him with word to another camp, and it was his job to get there as best he might.

The woods were full of dangers; so was the open. But the dread of all was the crocodiles in the river. Experience had taught the crocodiles that this was a favorite place for many kinds of prey to cross, and it was their custom to lie in wait for the chances offered.

Keeping out of sight himself, Crok looked well about. Then, grasping his stone club by the handle, with the thong slipped over his wrist, he dropped low, strode fast through the shallow water, came to the full, deep channel, plunged quietly, struck out with strong, sweeping strokes, and reached a rocky island in the middle. Quickly climbing up on this, he searched with his eye the current behind, before, and around him. No ripple was there to signal an enemy.

So, taking a good breath, he dived off the rock into the farther flood, swam under for a distance, came up, flung his dripping hair from his eyes, and silently struck out for the farther shore, where he landed in good time and glided out into the woods.

There, screened by the underbrush, he turned and studied the river, to see on the water two equal bumps a hand's-breadth apart, with the long ripple behind that stood for "crocodile." But Crok smiled gleefully, made a gesture of contempt, and strode along his proper trail.

It was a hundred thousand years later when next I saw Crok. He was standing in that very same position by the edge of a dangerous stream, peering up and down for lurking foes, before making a dash for the other side. He saw his chance; and, dashing, reached an iron-bound isle in the middle.

Then again he looked about; and, seeing an opening, sped safely to the other shore.

Yes, it was Crok again. The alertness and vigor were there. The sinewy limbs were there, but hidden in broadcloth. The jaw might be a trifle less square, but the eye was even brighter. The broad young shoulders were masked in linen and fur, and short curls were where the unkempt thatch once hung. But it was Crok, descendant of the same old Crok; with Crockers, Crocketts and McCrockens for kinfolk.

But the river now was a *crowded street,* with roaring motor-cars and reckless drivers; the island in the stream was hedged with iron posts, and a policeman made it safer. But the dangers were as great, the need for speed and nerve.

The gifts that made Crok win a hundred thousand years ago are his to-day—and his the victory too.

*from*

# Lonesome Dove

## Larry McMurtry

BY the middle of the afternoon it was so hot nobody could think. At least Newt couldn't, and the other hands didn't seem to be thinking very fast either. All they could find to argue about was whether it was hotter down in the well digging or up in the sun working the windlass. Down in the well they all worked so close together and sweated so much that it practically made a fog, while up in the sun fog was no problem. Being down in the well made Newt nervous, particularly if Pea was with him, because when Pea got to working the crowbar he didn't always look where he was jabbing and once had almost jabbed it through Newt's foot. From then on Newt worked spraddle-legged, so as to keep his feet out of the way.

They were going at it hard when the Captain came riding back, having lathered the mare good by loping her along the river for about twenty miles. He rode her right up to the well.

"Hello, boys," he said. "Ain't the water flowing yet?"

"It's flowin'," Dish said. "A gallon or two of it flowed outa me."

"Be thankful you're healthy," Call said. "A man that couldn't sweat would die in this heat."

"I don't suppose you'd trade for that mare," Dish asked. "I like her looks."

"You ain't the first that's liked them," Call said. "I'll keep her, I believe. But you boys can stop work now and catch a little rest. We have to go to Mexico tonight."

They all went over and sat in the alleyway of the barn—it had a little shade in it. The minute they sat down Deets began to patch his pants. He kept a big needle and some heavy thread in a cigar box in the saddle shed—given any chance he would get out his needle and start patching. He was woolly-headed and his wool was just getting gray.

"If I was you I'd give up on them pants," Dish said. "If you've got to wear quilts you best find a new one and start over."

"No, sir," Deets said genially. "These pants got to last."

Newt was a little excited. The Captain hadn't separated him

off from the rest of the men when he told them to rest. It might mean he was going to get to go to Mexico at last. On the other hand, he had been down in the well, so the Captain might just have forgotten him.

"I do fancy that mare," Dish said, watching the Captain unsaddle her.

"I don't see why," Pea said. "She near kilt the Captain just yesterday. Bit a hunk out of him the size of my foot."

They all looked at Pea's foot, which was about the size and shape of a scoop shovel.

"I'd say that passes belief," Dish said. "Her whole head ain't the size of your foot."

"If that chunk had come out of you you'd have thought it was big enough, I guess," Pea said mildly.

After Dish had caught his breath he pulled his case knife out of his pocket and asked if anyone wanted a game of root-the-peg. Newt had a pocketknife too and was quick to take him up. The game involved flipping the knives in various ways and making them stick in the dirt. Dish won and Newt had to dig a peg out of the ground with his teeth. Dish drove the peg in so far that Newt had dirt up his nose before he finally got it out.

The sight amused Pea no end. "By gosh, Newt, if we break the crowbar you can finish digging the well with your nose," he said.

While they were sitting around, idly experimenting with a few new knife throws, they heard the clop of horses and looked up to see two riders approaching from the east at an easy trot.

"Now who would that be?" Pea asked. "It's an odd time of day to visit."

"Well, if it ain't old Juan Cortinas it's probably just a couple of bank robbers," Dish said, referring to a Mexican cattle thief who was hailed, south of the river, as a great hero due to the success of his raids against the Texans.

"No, it ain't Cortinas," Pea Eye said, squinting at the riders. "He always rides a gray."

Dish could hardly believe anyone would be so dumb as to believe Juan Cortinas would just ride into Lonesome Dove with only one man.

The men stopped on the far side of the lots to read the sign Augustus had put up when the Hat Creek outfit had gone in business. All Call wanted on the sign was the simple words Hat Creek Livery Stable, but Augustus could not be persuaded to stop at a simple statement like that. It struck him that it would be best to put their rates on the sign. Call had been for tacking up one board with the name on it to let people know a livery stable was available, but Augustus thought that hopelessly unsophisticated; he bestirred himself and found an old plank door that had blown off somebody's root cellar, perhaps by the same wind that had taken their roof. He nailed the door onto one corner of the corrals, facing the road, so that the first thing most travelers saw when entering the town was the sign. In the end he and Call argued so much about what was to go on the sign that Call got disgusted and washed his hands of the whole project.

That suited Augustus fine, since he considered that he was the only person in Lonesome Dove with enough literary talent to write a sign. When the weather was fair he would go sit in the shade the sign cast and think of ways to improve it, in the two or three years since they had put it up he had thought of so many additions to the original simple declaration that practically the whole door was covered.

At first he had started out spare and just put the name of the firm, "Hat Creek Cattle Company and Livery Emporium," but that caused controversy in itself. Call claimed nobody knew what an emporium was, including himself, and he still didn't despite Augustus's many long-winded attempts to explain it to him. All Call knew was that they didn't run one, and he didn't want one, whatever it was, and there was no way something like that could fit with a cattle company.

However, Augustus had his way, and "Emporium" went on the sign. He mainly put it in because he wanted visitors to know there was at least one person in Lonesome Dove who knew how to spell important words.

Next he had put his name and Call's, his first because he was two years older and felt seniority should be honored. Call didn't care—his pride ran in other directions. Anyway he soon came to dislike the sign so much that he would just as soon not have had his name on it at all.

Pea Eye badly wanted his name on the sign, so one year Augustus lettered it in for him as a Christmas present. Pea, of course, couldn't read, but he could look, and once he got his name located on the sign he was quick to point it out to anyone who happened to be interested. He had already pointed it out to Dish, who wasn't interested particularly. Unfortunately it had been three decades since anyone had called Pea anything but Pea, and even Call, who had been the man to accept him into the Rangers, couldn't remember his real first name, though he knew his last name was Parker.

Having no wish to embarrass the man, Augustus had written him in as "P. E. Parker, Wrangler." He had wanted to list him as a blacksmith, since in truth Pea was a superior blacksmith and only an average wrangler, but Pea Eye thought he could sit a horse as well as anyone and didn't wish to be associated publicly with a lower trade.

Newt recognized that he was rightly too young to have his name on the sign and never suggested the possibility to anyone, though it would have pleased him mightily if someone had suggested it for him. No one did, but then Deets had to wait nearly two years before his name appeared on the sign, and Newt resigned himself to waiting too.

Of course, it had not occurred to Augustus to put Deets's name on, Deets being a black man. But when Pea's name was added there was a lot of discussion about it, and around that time Deets developed a tremendous case of the sulks—unlike him and perplexing to Call. Deets had ridden with him for years, through all weathers and all dangers, over country so barren they had more than once had to kill a horse to have meat, and in all those years Deets had given cheerful service. Then, all because of the sign, he went into a sulk and stayed in it until Augustus finally spotted him looking wistfully at it one day and figured it out. When Augustus told Call about his conclusion, Call was further outraged. "That damn sign's ruint this outfit," he said, and went into a sulk himself. He had known Augustus was vain but would never have suspected Deets or Pea of such a failing.

Of course Augustus was happy to add Deets's name to the sign, although, as in the case of Pea, there was some trouble with the particulars. Simply writing "Deets" on the sign didn't work. Deets couldn't read either, but he could see that his name was far too short in comparison with the others. At least it was short in comparison with the other names on the sign, and Deets wanted to know why.

"Well, Deets, you just got one name," Augustus said. "Most people got two. Maybe you've got two and just forgot one of them."

Deets sat around thinking for a day or two, but he could not remember ever having another name, and Call's recollection bore him out. At that point even Augustus began to think the sign was more trouble than it was worth, since it was turning out to be so hard to please everyone. The only solution was to think up another name to go with Deets, but while they were debating various possibilities, Deets's memory suddenly cleared.

"Josh," he said, one night after supper, to the surprise of everyone. "Why, I'm Josh. Can you write that, Mr. Gus?"

"Josh is short for Joshua," Augustus said. "I can write either one of them. Joshua's the longest."

"Write the longest," Deets said. "I'm too busy for a short name."

That made no particular sense, nor were they ever able to get Deets to specify how he happened to remember that Josh was his other name. Augustus wrote him on the sign as "Deets, Joshua," since he had already written the "Deets." Fortunately Deets's vanity did not extend to needing a title, although Augustus was tempted to write him in as a prophet—it would have gone with "Joshua," but Call had a fit when he mentioned it.

"You'll have us the laughingstock of this whole county," Call said. "Suppose somebody come up to Deets and asked him to prophesy?"

Deets himself thought that was an amusing prospect. "Why, I could do it, Captain," he said. "I'd prophesy hot and I'd prophesy dry and I'd charge 'em a dime."

Once the names were settled the rest of the sign was a simple matter. There were two categories, things for rent and things for sale. Horses and rigs were available for rental, or at least horses and one rig, a spring buggy with no springs that they had bought from Xavier Wanz after his wife, Therese, had got smashed by it. For sale Augustus listed cattle and horses. As an afterthought he added, "Goats and Donkey's Neither Bought nor Sold," since he had no patience with goats and Call even less with donkeys. Then, as another afterthought, he had added, "We Don't Rent Pigs," which occasioned yet another argument with Call.

"Why, they'll think we're crazy here when they see that," he said. "Nobody in their right mind would want to rent a pig. What would you do with a pig once you rented it?"

"Why, there's plenty of useful tasks pigs can do," Augustus said. "They could clean the snakes out of a cellar, if a man had a cellar. Or they can soak up mud puddles. Stick a few pigs in a mud puddle and pretty soon the puddle's gone."

It was a burning day, and Call was sweated down. "If I could find anything as cool as a mud puddle I'd soak it up myself," he said.

"Anyhow, Call, a sign's a kind of a tease," Augustus said. "It ought to make a man stop and consider just what it is he wants out of life in the next few days."

"If he thinks he wants to rent a pig he's not a man I'd want for a customer," Call said.

The caution about pigs ended the sign to Augustus's satisfaction, at least for a while, but after a year or two had passed, he decided it would add dignity to it all if the sign ended with a Latin motto. He had an old Latin schoolbook that had belonged to his father; it was thoroughly battered from having been in his saddlebags for years. It had a few pages of mottoes in the back, and Augustus spent many happy hours poring over them, trying to decide which might look best at the bottom of the sign. Unfortunately the mottoes had not been translated, perhaps because by the time the students got to the back of the book they were supposed to be able to read Latin. Augustus had had only a fleeting contact with the language and had no real opportunity to improve his knowledge; once he had been caught in an ice storm on the plains and had torn out a number of pages of the grammar in order to get a fire started. He had kept himself from freezing, but at the cost of most of the grammar and vocabulary; what was left didn't help him much with the mottoes at the end of the book. However, it was his view that Latin was mostly for looks anyway, and he devoted himself to the mottoes in order to find one with the best look. The one he settled on was *Uva uvam vivendo varia fit*, which seemed to him a beautiful motto, whatever it meant. One day when nobody was around he went out and lettered it onto the bottom of the sign, just below "We Don't Rent Pigs." Then he felt that his handiwork was complete. The whole sign read:

HAT CREEK CATTLE COMPANY
AND LIVERY EMPORIUM

CAPT. AUGUSTUS MC CRAE ⎫
CAPTAIN W. F. CALL ⎭ PROPS.

P. E. PARKER                WRANGLER

DEETS, JOSHUA

FOR RENT: HORSES AND RIGS

FOR SALE: CATTLE AND HORSES

GOATS AND DONKEY'S NEITHER BOUGHT NOR SOLD

WE DON'T RENT PIGS.

*UVA UVAM VIVENDO VARIA FIT.*

Augustus didn't say a word about the motto, and it was a good two months before anybody even noticed it, which showed how unobservant the citizens of Lonesome Dove really were. It galled Augustus severely that no one appreciated the fact that he had thought to write a Latin motto on a sign that all visitors could see as they rode in, though in fact those riding in took as little note of it as those already in, perhaps because getting to Lonesome Dove was such a hot, exhausting business. The few people who accomplished it were in no mood to stop and study erudite signs.

More galling still was the fact that no member of his own firm had noticed the motto, not even Newt, from whom Augustus expected a certain alertness. Of course two members of the firm were totally illiterate—three, if he chose to count Bolivar—and wouldn't have known Latin from Chinese. Still, the way they casually treated the sign as just part of the landscape caused Augustus to brood a good deal about the contempt that familiarity breeds.

*from*

# The Narrative of the Expedition of Coronado

## Pedro de Castañeda

*Coronado and his men set off to find the fabled Native American city of Quivira, in the southwestern plains. Their guide, Turk, a plains Indian who cooperated with the Spanish in exchange for a promise of freedom, leads them far off course into central Texas.*

THE general started from the ravine with the guides that the Teyas had given him. He appointed the alderman Diego Lopez his army-master, and took with him the men who seemed to him to be most efficient, and the best horses. . . .

The general arrived—I mean, the guides ran away during the first few days and Diego Lopez had to return to the army for guides, bringing orders for the army to return to Tiguex to find food and wait there for the general. The Teyas, as before, willingly furnished him with new guides. The army waited for its messengers and spent a fortnight here, preparing jerked beef to take with them. It was estimated that during this fortnight they killed 500 bulls. The number of these that were there without any cows was something incredible. Many fellows were lost at this time who went out hunting and did not get back to the army for two or three days, wandering about the country as if they were crazy, in one direction or another, not knowing how to get back where they started from, although this ravine extended in either direction so that they could find it. Every night they took account of who was missing, fired guns and blew trumpets and beat drums and built great fires, but yet some of them went off so far and wandered about so much that all this did not give them any help, although it helped others. The only way was to go back where they had killed an animal and start from there in one direction and another until they struck the ravine or fell in with somebody who could put them on the right road. It is worth noting that the country there is so level that at midday, after one has wandered about in one direction and another in pursuit of game, the only thing to do is to stay near the game quietly until sunset, so as to see where it goes down, and even then they have to be men who are practiced to do it. Those who are not, had to trust themselves to others.

The general followed his guides until he reached Quivira, which took forty-eight days' marching, on account of the great detour they had made toward Florida. He was received peacefully on account of the guides whom he had. They asked the Turk why he had lied and had guided them so far out of their way. He said that his country was in that direction and that, besides this, the people at Cicuye had asked him to lead them off on to the plains and lose them, so that the horses would die when their provisions gave out, and they would be so weak if they ever returned that they would be killed without any trouble, and thus they could take revenge for what had been done to them. This was the reason why he had led them astray, supposing that they did not know how to hunt or to live without corn, while as for the gold, he did not know where there was any of it. He said this like one who had given up hope and who found that he was being persecuted, since they had begun to believe Ysopete who had guided them better than he had, and fearing lest those who were there might give some advice by which some harm would come to him. . . .

The messengers whom the army had sent to the general returned, as I said, and then, as they brought no news except what the alderman had delivered, the army left the ravine and returned to the Teyas, where they took guides who led them back by a more direct road. They readily furnished these, because these people are always roaming over this country in pursuit of the animals and so know it thoroughly. They keep their road in this way: In the morning they notice where the sun rises and observe the direction they are going to take, and then shoot an arrow in this direction. Before reaching this they shoot another over it, and in this way they go all day toward the water where they are to end the day. In this way they covered in 25 days what had taken them 37 days going, besides stopping to hunt cows on the way. They found many salt lakes on this road, and there was a great quantity of salt. There were thick pieces of it on top of the water bigger than tables, as thick as four or five fingers. Two or three spans down under water there was salt which tasted better than that in the floating pieces, because this was rather bitter. It was crystalline. All over these plains there were large numbers of animals like squirrels and a great number of their holes.

On its return the army reached the Cicuye river more than 30 leagues below there—I mean below the bridge they had made when they crossed it, and they followed it up to that place. In general, its banks are covered with a sort of rose bushes, the fruit of which tastes like muscatel grapes. They grow on little twigs about as high up as a man. It has the parsley leaf. There were unripe grapes and currants and wild marjoram. The guides said this river joined that of Tiguex more than 20 days from here, and that its course turned toward the east. It is believed that it flows into the mighty river of the Holy Spirit which the men with Don Hernando de Soto discovered in Florida. A painted Indian woman ran away from Juan de Saldibar and hid in the ravines about this time, because she recognized the country of Tiguex where she had been a slave. She fell into the hands of some Spaniards who had entered the country from Florida to explore it in this direction. After I got back to New Spain I heard them say that the Indian told them that she had run away from other men like them nine days, and that she gave the names of some captains; from which we ought to believe that we were not far from the region they discovered, although they said they were more than 200 leagues inland. I believe the land at that point is more than *600 leagues* across from sea to sea.

As I said, the army followed the river up as far as Cicuye, which it found ready for war and unwilling to make any advances toward peace or to give any food to the army. From there they went on to Tiguex where several villages had been reinhabited, but the people were afraid and left them again.

# Tejanos' Petition to the Mexican Government

Honorable Congress

When illnesses occur, the treatment adopted should be proportionate to the gravity of the situation, and application should be immediate. Such is the only rule to be followed when the physical body is attacked by some severe illness. To be consistent, the same procedure should be followed when dealing with ailments of the social body. No doubt exists that ills, similar in nature, have afflicted each of the unfortunate towns of Texas from the very moment they were founded. So it is that some towns have been destroyed while the rest have been unable to attain, even for a single day, that peace or those other guarantees which should have insured . . . development under the paternal protection of their governments. This town of Béxar was established 140 years ago, La Bahía del Espíritu Santo and Nacogdoches 116 years ago, and the fort of San Sabá, the towns of Jaén, San Marcos, and Trinidad, were founded in the intervening years along with other military establishments on the Guadalupe, Colorado and Brazos rivers. These communities have disappeared entirely; in some of them the residents dying to the last man. . . . Many early settlers and their descendants have been sacrificed to the barbarians, and not a few others have died of hunger and pestilence, which have caused havoc in this part of the republic due to the inaction and apathy of those who govern. How sad that ninety-seven men have been murdered by Indians within the limits of this city [San Antonio], Bahía, and the new *villa* of González alone . . . Other frontier communities, located toward the west have, perhaps, suffered much more, and every last one of us is probably threatened with total extermination by the new Comanche uprising. This very large and most warlike tribe renewed hostilities four months ago . . .

These disturbances have caused us to suffer absolute poverty. Since the troops protecting this part of the frontier have not received even one-tenth part of their salary during the entire past year, it has been necessary to put more than half of them at liberty so they would find means for their own subsistence. Today, in all of Texas, only seventy men are at arms. Their pay in arrears, these troops are a burden on the poor townspeople. To assure themselves that even this limited support will remain available, the poor townspeople are obliged to supply these men with grain and other essential articles from the already meager community resources. . . .

Experience suggests that the first colonization law of this state contains many omissions and contradictions. These have paralyzed population growth in Texas and, because of them, elements of its territorial wealth have failed to develop. . . .

On the other hand, what inducement, what incentives, or what privileges capable of attracting Mexicans have been written into that or any later law designed to encourage an increase in the population of Mexicans (who doubtless would be the most desirable citizens for Texas)? Not even one. On the contrary, the May 2, 1832 law establishes that lands in Texas are priced at from one to three hundred pesos, according to their quality, while those of Coahuila at only fifteen pesos. What an admirable measure! Principally it serves to keep the Mexican population at a greater distance from Texas, because people from the interior of the Republic have always resisted immigrating to these deserts which they greatly fear. Very few Mexican residents of Texas will be able to afford the indicated fees because of their limited capital. . . .

And what shall we say concerning evils caused by the general law of April 6, 1830, which absolutely prohibits immigration by North Americans? The lack of troops and other officials capable of supervising it has made it impossible to enforce this law. On the other hand, the law prevents immigration of some capitalists and of some industrious and honorable men who have refrained from coming because of it, but has left the door open to wicked adventurers and others who constitute the dregs of society. Since they have nothing to lose, they have arrived furtively in large numbers and may cause incalculable harm.

The same is true of the numerous tribes of semicivilized Indians. Expelled from the United States of North America, they have crossed the Sabine River and, unchallenged, have established themselves in our territory. It will be very difficult to uproot them and even more so if we intend to make them observe our legal system. Yet, risking all kinds of dangers and inconveniences, North Americans reclaimed a considerable part of these lands from the desert prior to the passage of the law of April 6, 1830, and toiled assiduously to further agriculture and to introduce crafts unknown in these parts since the discovery of this land by the old Spanish government. They planted cotton and sugar cane, introduced the cotton gin, and imported machinery for the cultivation of sugar and sawmills to cut wood economically. We owe these advances to the efforts of these hard-working colonists, who have earned a comfortable living within seven or eight years. Theirs is not a precarious existence, the only kind known in Mexican towns, which depend solely upon the troops' payroll that circulates so slowly among us.

Although it grieves us to say so, we should state that the miserable manufacture of blankets, hats, and even shoes was never established in Texas towns. Lack of these articles has obliged us to beg them from foreigners or from the interior of the republic, two or three hundred leagues distant. The only known loom here is one brought to Béxar two years ago. Meanwhile, residents of La Bahía and Nacogdoches who have never left their communities have no idea of this very simple machine, or the way a hat is made. All these resources came to us with the North American colonists, but if their immigration is blocked who knows how long we will be denied such advances.

Immigration is, unquestionably, the most efficient, quick, and economical means we can employ to destroy the Indians and to populate lands they now occupy—directing the immigrants to the northern interior whenever possible. This goal can only be achieved by freely admitting these enthusiastic North Americans so they may live in this desert. They already are experienced in dealing with the barbarians in their native land, where they have done similar work. Not a single European nation that might be interested in colonizing offers their people similar advantages. Because they have been very regimented, the Europeans' transportation, climate, customs, and forms of government are very different from those of the neighboring republic and are not as suitable for Mexico.

The opening of roads going directly from Texas ports to New Mexico, Paso del Norte, or even Chihuahua, would place Texas at the rank it should occupy in the Mexican federation. This achievement, too, is the result of the immigration of North American capitalists. They built these at least more economically and in less time than could be accomplished by any other nation and even by Mexico itself. The same is true of direct communication from all the far northern part of our republic with the state of

Missouri of the neighboring nation, which is maintained today despite great risk and cost of freight. The population of those lands [between Texas and Missouri, and between Texas and New Mexico] would benefit Texas and would be the best barrier against the Indians. . . .

The advantages that would accrue to this part of the republic, if it could be populated without need of sacrifice by the public treasury or the state, are so numerous they are hard to imagine. Perhaps an entire volume would be insufficient to provide full and minute details of such a beautiful scene. And would not the inhabitants of Texas find it painful and even intolerable to continue envisioning how easily prosperity could be attained in this fertile land . . . and for these settlers to realize that only the government's lack of knowledge and the mistaken measures it undertook to encourage population in this country increasingly separate us from the well-being to which nature invites us? This same apathy and the fatal arrow of the barbarians will probably deprive us of our existence as they did our forebears. Unquestionably, the lack of a government with special sensitivity to the needs of Texas, which would take the necessary and simple measures to increase Texas' population and promote its prosperity and growth in all branches, has been, is, and perhaps will continue to be the source of our suffering.

# The Importance of Dancing to Early Texans

## William Ransom Hogan

NO pastime in American history has been carried out with more unstinted gusto than frontier dancing. A Texas woman explained how it met the psychological requirements for a Western diversion:

Times were too pregnant with excitement for grave pleasures to take strong hold of the minds of the people. . . . How could people sit often to listen to grave discourses when at every random shot of a gun their ears were on the alert for the cry of Indians. To be so situated as to have these quick vibrations operate nervously upon the brain predisposes the mind to seek relief in softer emotions of pleasure, but still one of excitement, consequently the dancing master found favor with the majority instead of the philosopher.

Dances were held on every possible occasion, even after funerals, and the scarcity of women only accentuated the frontier passion for dancing. In 1839 a young man wrote: "We had three balls in Bastrop lately. . . . I paid but little attention to the ladies, contenting myself with a little girl about 11 years old for my partner. The men were so crazey [sic] after the grown up ladies that I never interfered with them." To these dances, as was customary, mothers brought their babies, wrapped them in shawls and blankets, and left them beneath the temporary benches along the walls while they participated in the merriment. Stephen F. Austin once found his sister Emily "at a ball dancing away in fine spirits," when her baby was not six weeks old.

A single violinist customarily provided the music and many Negroes fiddled their way into white folks' favor. But the lack of a musician was often a serious problem. A contemporary newspaper story told by an army captain who had found dancers in an East Texas tavern attempting to revive the only available fiddler, victim of an overdose of inspiration from his whiskey bottle, contains a genuine appraisal of this common problem. "The dancers," so went the story, "rolled the drunken man upon the floor, they stirred him up, they rubbed his head with vinegar, and they crammed an

entire jar of Underwood's pickles down his throat—but all would
not do." Although the captain had never played any sort of musical
instrument, he offered to substitute for the drunken musician.
When the dancers accepted enthusiastically, the captain took his
place in the violinist's chair, picked up the fiddle, and made a few
musicianlike flourishes and preliminary motions.

Once or twice he drew the bow scientifically across the strings,
which were now horribly out of tune—flourishes which caused
the eager dancers immediately to commence "forwarding" across
the floor—but the waggish captain had no intention of giving
them a "send off" so suddenly.

At length, he drew the cork by giving every string on the violin
a general rake with the bow. Away they went like mad, Captain
H. still sawing away, stamping his right foot as if keeping time,
and calling the figure. . . . series of sounds came from the pun-
ished violin which would set a professor crazy; but so full of
dance were the head and foot couple that they carried the thing
with as much zeal as though they had been bitten by Italian
tarantulas.

It may readily be supposed that the dancers had but a limited
knowledge of music; but still they could tell, in their cooler mo-
ments, a tune from a tornado. The first two couple[s] had by
this time finished, and the second had commenced, when one of
the former addressed his partner with:

"Eliza, did you ever hear that tune he's aplaying afore?"

"Can't say that I ever has," was the response, and this within
hearing of Captain H. who was still punishing the violin as severely as ever.

"Does it sound to you like much of a tune . . . any how?"

"Well, it doesn't."

"Nor to me either," said the first speaker, who all the while had
his head turned to one side after the manner of a hog listening.
"My opinion is that that feller there is naterally jest sawin away
without exactly knowing what he's a doin."

This was too much for the captain, who now dropped the violin and rushed from the room and sought his quarters for the
night. Thus ended a ball in Eastern Texas.

Other accounts of dances are more definitely descriptive. From
them it is clear that it was no drawback that a log cabin floor was
made of puncheons [wood] or consisted of bare earth. Even as the

prevailing type of women's skirts has influenced dance styles in modern times, so the roughness of cabin floors made smooth dances impossible. As one settler said, "When young folks danced in those days, they danced; they didn't glide around; they 'shuffled' and 'double shuffled,' 'wired' and 'cut the pigeon's wing' making the splinters fly." After the men with boots had danced awhile, they exchanged their footgear for the moccasins worn by their less fortunate companions, who were thus enabled to take the floor and make the proper amount of noise. If "the din of clattering feet" drowned out the music of the fiddler as he played "Molly Cotton-Tail," "Munny Musk," or "Leather Breeches," his efforts were often supplemented by those of other musicians using crude instruments such as a clevis, hoe and case knife, or a tin pan.

In the larger towns and on a few plantations, many balls were conducted with a certain amount of style. The graceful performance of the cotillions and reels of the day were taught by the few dancing masters who found their way to Texas; among these was "Mon. Amadee Grignon" who charged the citizens of Houston and Galveston one dollar per lesson. The presence of these teachers is only another small addition to the record which shows a considerable amount of dancing in the Republic. A dance in a town was attended by practically the whole population—and a failure to receive an invitation might be the cause for a challenge to a duel.

There is little evidence that dancing met with the strong religious objections which were a part of the prevailing moral code in many Texas communities after the country became more settled. A Methodist circuit rider wrote from the village of Montgomery in 1843 that he had gone three fourths of the way around his circuit and found "nothing cheering, or encouraging, many of the members having backslidden and are spiritually dead—some have been going to dancing school, and some have joined the Baptists!" But few preachers crusaded against dancing; most of them were merely lukewarm on the subject; and at least one played the violin and even danced himself. The truth seems to have been that they found evils more pernicious to combat in excessive gambling, fighting, swearing, and misuse of the Lord's Day. Even if they had been inclined to preach against square dancing, their condemnation may not have been effective because the membership of the churches, liberally estimated, did not constitute one fourth of the population. Furthermore, the frequence of dances points to a strong public sentiment supporting the amusement.

# *from* A Teenage Bride on the Santa Fe Trail

## Susan Shelby Magoffin

*CAMP No. 18 On the wide Prairie. Sunday June 28th, 1846.* This is my third Sabbath on the Plains. And how does conscience tell me it has been spent? Oh, may my heavenly father grant me pardon for my wickedness! Did I not in the very beginning of it forget—yes, and how can I be pardoned for the great sin—that it was the Holy Sabbath, appointed by my heavenly father for a day of rest—and classed it so much with the days of the week, that I regularly took out my week's work, kniting. Oh, how could I ever have been so thoughtless, so unmindful of my duty and my eternal salvation!

Passed the whole day with little wood, and no water for the cattle, but some little about in puddles. Had some difficulty in crossing a swampy place, this evening; the teamsters [people driving the wagons] had to mow grass and put in it, before they could pass their teams.

*Noon. No. 20. Little Arkansas River. June 30th, 1846.* Come my feeble pen, put on thy specks and assist this full head to unburthen itself! Thou hast a longer story than is usual to tell. How we left *Camp No. 19* yesterday (Monday) morning after a sleepless night, our tent was pitched in the musquito region and when will the God Somnus [sleep] make his appearance in such quarters? It was slap, slap, all the time, from one party of the combatants, while the others came with a buz and a bite.

We traveled till 11 o'clock with the hope of finding water for the weary cattle. The sun was excessively oppressive. Col. Owens' mule teams left us entirely, but his oxen like ours were unable to stand the heat. They were before us and stoped—we followed their example, as much from necessity as any thing else. The oxen, some of them staggered under their yokes, and when we turned out for want of water—there was none within five miles of us that we knew of—some of the most fatigued absolutely crept under the wagons for shade, and did not move till they were driven up in the evening. One poor thing fell in the road and we almost gave him up for lost. His driver though, rather a tender hearted lad I presume, went with a bucket to a *mud hole* and brought the *wet mud* which was a little cool, and *plastered his body over with it.* He then got all the water from the water kegs after the men had drank, which was not more than two or three tin cups full; he took this and opening the ox's mouth poured it down his throat. He then made a covering over him with ox yokes standing up and blankets spread over. In the course of an hour or two the poor thing could get up, and walk. But his great thirst for water led him to searching the deep grass, and when the wagons started at 5 o'clock, he could not be found. Roman, the old Mexican who attended the loose stock, hunted some time for him, but to no purpose. Other sick ones needed his attention and it was probable this one had gone back to last night's camp ground, and as it was too far to send on an uncertainty and pressing times, we gave up the search.

It blew up a little cooler towards sunset and we travelled pretty well, to make water was our object; both man and beast were craving it. The former could occasionally find a little to quench his parched thirst, by searching ravines that were grown up with tall weeds, this tho' muddy, and as warm as a scorching sun beaming into it all day could make it, was a luxurious draught [drink]. Now, about dark, we came into the musquito regions, and I found to my great *horror* that I have been complaining all this time for nothing, yes absolutely for *nothing;* for some two or hundred or even thousands are nothing compared with what we now encountered. The carriage mules became so restless that they passed all the wagons and switching their tails from side to side, as fast as they could, and slaping their ears, required some strength of our Mexican driver to hold them in. He would jerk the reins and exclaim *"hola los animal[es] como estande bravos!"* [Ho, animals! how wild you are!] The moon was not very bright and we could not see far before us. Suddenly one of the mules sprang to one side, reared, and pitched till I really believed we should turn over. Magoffin discouvered something lying in the road, and springing from the carriage pulled me out. It was a dead ox lying immediately in our way, and it is no wonder the mule was frightened.

In my own hurry to get out I had entirely forgotten the musquitoes, and on returning to the carriage I found my feet covered with stings, and my dress full, where they had gotten on me in the grass. About 10 o'clock we came upon a dark ravine, over which *las caras* [*los carros*—the wagons] would probably experience some difficulty in passing, so we stoped to see them over. The mules became perfectly frantic, and nothing could make them stand. They were turned out to shift for themselves, and Magoffin seeing no other alternative than to remain there all night, tied his head and neck up with pocket handkerchiefs and set about having the tent stretched. I drew my feet up under me, wraped my shawl over my head, till I almost smothered with heat, and listened to the din without. And such a noise as it was, I shall pray ever to be preserved. Millions upon millions were swarming around me, and their knocking against the carriage *reminded me of a hard rain.* It was equal to any of the plagues of Egypt [the torments sent by God to convince the Egyptians to release the Israelites]. I lay almost in a perfect stupor, the heat and stings made me perfectly sick, till Magoffin came to the carriage and told me to *run if I could,* with my shawl, bonnet and shoes on (and without opening my mouth, Jane said, for they would *choke* me) straight to the bed. When I got there they pushed me straight in under the musquito bar, which had been tied up in some kind of a fashion, and oh, dear, what a relief it was to breathe again. There I sat in my cage, like an imprisoned creature frightened half to death.

Magoffin now rolled himself up some how with all his cloths on, and lay down at my side, he dare not raise the bar to get in. I tried to sleep and towards daylight succeeded. On awaking this morning I found my forehead, arms and feet covered with knots. They were not little red places as musquitos generally make, but they were knots, some of them quite as large as a pea. We knocked up [took down] the tent as quick as possible and without thinking of breakfast came off to this place, passing on our way our own wagons and those of Col. Owens encamped at Mud Creek.

On our arrival here the buffalo [robe] and pillow were spread out and I layed down to sleep and I can say it took no rocking to accomplish the end. The tent was stretched with the intention of remaining here all night. The crossing is quite difficult, the sun extremely warm and it was supposed the oxen could not go on. About 11 o'clock *mi alma* [literally "my heart," referring to her husband] came and raised me by my hand entirely up onto my feet without waking me. The whole scene had entirely changed. The sky was perfectly dark, wind blowing high, the atmosphere cool and pleasant and *no musquitoes,* with every appearance of a hard storm.

At 12 o'clock breakfast was ready, and after drinking a cup of tea I fell on the bed completely worn out. After two or three hours sound sleep I got up washed, combed my head, put on clean cloths—a luxury on the plains by the way—and sallied forth in the cool air somewhat refreshed. I brought out my writing implements and here I am.

. . . *July 4th 1846. Pawnee Fork. Saturday.* What a disasterous *celebration* I have today. It is certainly the greatest miracle that I have my head on my shoulders. I think I can never forget it if I live to be as old as my grandmother.

The wagons left Pawnee Rock some time before us.—For I was anxious to see this wonderful curiosity. We went up and while *mi alma* with his gun and pistols kept watch, for the wily Indian may always be apprehended here, it is a good lurking place and they are ever ready to fall upon any unfortunate trader behind his company—and it is necessary to be careful, so while *mi alma* watched on the rock above and Jane stood by to watch if any should come up on the front side of me, I cut my name, among the many hundreds inscribed on the rock and many of whom I knew. It was not done well, for fear of Indians made me tremble all over and I hurried it over in any way. This I remarked would be quite an adventure to celebrate the 4th! but woe betide I have yet another to relate.

The wagons being some distance ahead we rode on quite briskly to overtake them. In an hour's time we had driven some six miles, and at *Ash creek* we came up with them. No water in the creek and the crossing pretty good only a tolerably steep bank on the first side of it, all but two had passed over, and as these were not up we drove on ahead of them to cross first. The bank though a little steep was smooth and there could be no difficulty in riding down it.—However, we had made up our minds always to walk down such places in case of accident, and before we got to it *mi alma* hallowed "woe" as he always does when he wishes to stop, but as there was no motion made by the driver to that effect, he repeated it several times and with much vehemence [force]. We had now reached the very verge [edge] of the cliff and seeing it a good way and apparently less dangerous than jumping out as we were, he said "go on." The word was scarcely from his lips, ere we were whirled completely over with a perfect crash. One to see the wreck of that carriage now with the top and sides entirely broken to pieces, could never believe that people had come out of it alive. But strange, wonderful to say, we are almost entirely unhurt! I was considerably stunned at first and could not stand on my feet. *Mi alma* forgetting himself and entirely enlisted for my safety carried me in his arms to a shade tree, almost entirely without my knowledge, and rubing my face and hands with whiskey soon brought me entire to myself.—My back and side are a little hurt, but is very small compared with what it might have been. *Mi alma* has his left hip and arm on which he fell both bruised and strained, but not seriously. Dear creature 'twas for me he received this, for had he not caught me in his arms as we fell he could have saved himself entirely. And then I should perhaps have been killed or much crushed for the top fell over me, and it was only his hands that kept it off of me. It is better as it is, for we can sympathise more fully with each other.

It was a perfect mess that; of people, books, bottles—one of which broke, and on my head too I believe—guns, pistols, baskets, bags, boxes and the dear knows what else. I was insensible to it all except when something gave me a hard knock and brought me to myself. We now sought refuge in Jane's carriage for our own could only acknowledge its incapability.

*from*

# Eyewitness to the Alamo

## Bill Groneman

### by Enrique Esparza, May 12 and May 19, 1907

*This account of Enrique Esparza comes to us from Charles Merritt Barnes (1855–1927), a reporter for the* San Antonio Express. *Barnes began working for the paper about 1880. It is likely that the many articles published about Alamo survivors and witnesses between this time and the early 1900s could be attributed to Barnes even if he did not receive a byline for some of them. . . . Esparza is described in the 1907 article as being twelve years old at the time of the battle.*

YOU ask me do I remember it. I tell you yes. It is burned into my brain and indelibly seared there. Neither age nor infirmity could make me forget, for the scene was one of such horror that it could never be forgotten by any one who witnessed the incidents. . . .

I was then a boy of 12 years of age; was then quite small and delicate and could have passed for a child of 8. My father was a friend and comrade of William Smith. Smith had expected to send my father and our family away with his own family in a wagon to Nacogdoches. We were waiting for the wagon to be brought to town. My father and Smith had heard of the approach of Santa Anna, but did not expect him and his forces to arrive as early as they did. Santa Anna and his men got there before the wagon we waited for could come.

My father was told by Smith that all who were friends to the Americans had better join the Americans who had taken refuge in the Alamo. Smith and his family were there and my father and his family went with them.

Santa Anna and his army arrived at about sundown and almost immediately after we sought refuge in the Alamo. Immediately after their arrival Santa Anna's personal staff dismounted on Main Plaza in front of the San Fernando church. Santa Anna went into the building at the northwest corner of Main Plaza which has been superseded by that now occupied by S. Wolfson. That building had been occupied by the Texans and before them by the soldiers of Mexico and still earlier by the soldiers of Spain. It had been a part of the presidio or old fort, and the part where the officers had their headquarters. The Texans had left his structure and gone over to the Alamo because the latter offered more advantages for defense.

I have often heard it said that Santa Anna immediately upon his arrival in San Antonio dismounted in the West side of Military Plaza and hitched his horse to an iron ring set into the wall of the old building where the Spanish Governors dwelt and where the combined coats of arms of Spain and Austria form the keystone of the arch above its portal. This is not so, I saw Santa Anna when he arrived. I saw him dismount. He did not hitch the horse. He gave its bridle reins to a lackey. He and his staff proceeded immediately to the house on the Northwest corner of Main Plaza. I was playing with some other children on the Plaza and when Santa Anna and his soldiers came up we ran off and told our parents, who almost immediately afterward took me and the other children of the family to the Alamo. I am sure of this for I saw Santa Anna several times afterward and after I came out of the Alamo.

It was twilight when we got into the Alamo and it grew pitch dark soon afterward. All of the doors were closed and barred. The sentinels that had been on duty without were first called inside and then the openings closed. Some sentinels were posted up on the roof, but those were protected by the walls of the Alamo church and the old Convent building. We went into the church portion. It was shut up when we arrived. We were admitted through a small window.

I distinctly remember that I climbed through the window and over a cannon that was placed inside of the church immediately behind the window. There were several other cannon there. Some were back of the doors. Some had been mounted on the roof and some had been placed in the Convent. The window was opened to permit us to enter and it was closed immediately after we got inside.

We had not been in there long when a messenger came from Santa Anna calling on us to surrender. I remember the reply to this summons was a shot from one of the cannon on the roof of the Alamo. Soon after it was fired I heard Santa Anna's cannon reply. I heard his cannon shot strike the walls of the church and also the Convent. Then I heard the cannon within the Alamo buildings, both church and Convent, fire repeatedly during the night. I heard the cheers of the Alamo gunners and the deriding jeers of Santa Anna's troops.

My heart quaked when the shot tore through the timbers. My fear and terror was overwhelming but my brave mother and my dauntless father sought to soothe and quiet my brothers and myself. My sister was but an infant and knew naught of the tragic scenes enacted about us. But even child as I was I could not help but feel inspired by the bravery of the heroes about me.

If I had been given a weapon I would have fought likewise. But weapons and ammunition were scarce and only wielded and used by those who knew how. But I saw some there no older than I who had them and fought as bravely and died as stolidly as the adults. This was towards the end and when many of the grown persons within had been slain by the foes without. It was then that some of the children joined in the defense.

All who had weapons used them as often as they had the chance to do so. Shots were fired fast. Bullets flew thick. Both men and women fell within the walls. Even children died there. The fighting was intermittent. We must have been within the Alamo 10 or 12 days. I did not count the days. But they were long and full of terror. The nights were longer and fraught with still more horror. It was between the period of fierce fighting and all too short armistice that we got any rest.

Crockett seemed to be the leading spirit. He was everywhere. He went to every exposed point and personally directed the fighting. Travis was chief in command, but he depended more upon the judgment of Crockett and that brave man's intrepidity than upon his own. Bowie, too, was brave and dauntless, but he was ill. Prone upon his cot he was unable to see much that was going on about him and the others were too engrossed to stop and tell him. Although too weak to stand upon his feet, when Travis drew the line with his sword Bowie had those around him bring his cot across the line.

I heard the few Mexicans there call Crockett "Don Benito." Afterward I learned his name was David, but I only knew him as "Don Benito."

One day when I went to where Bowie was lying on his cot I heard him call those about him and say:

"All of you who desire to leave here may go in safety. Santa Anna has just sent a message to Travis saying there will be an armistice for 3 days to give us time to deliberate on surrendering. During these 3 days all who desire to do so may go out of here. Travis has sent me the message and told me to tell those near me."

When Bowie said this quite a number left. Travis and Bowie took advantage of this occasion to send out for succor they vainly hoped would come to the Alamo and those within before it fell. William Smith and Alsberry [*sic*] were among those who were sent for succor then, Seguin claimed also to have been so sent. Among the surnames of those I remember to have left during the time of this armistice were Menchaca, Flores, Rodrigues, Ramirez, Arocha, Silvero. They are now all dead. Among the women who went out were some of their relatives.

Rose left after this armistice had expired and after the others had been sent for succor. Rose went out after Travis drew the line with his sword. He was the only man who did not cross the line. Up to then he had fought as bravely as any man there. He had stood by the cannon.

Rose went out during the night. They opened a window for him and let him go. The others who left before went out of the doors and in the daytime. Alsberry [*sic*] left his wife and sister-in-law there. His sister-in-law afterward married a man named Cantu. She and Mrs. Alsberry [*sic*] stayed in the Alamo until it fell. They feared to leave, believing the Mexicans under Santa Anna would kill them.

Bowie asked my father if he wished to go when the armistice of 3 days was on. My father replied:

"No, I will stay and die fighting." My mother then said:

"I will stay by your side and with our children die too. They will soon kill us. We will not linger in pain."

So we stayed. And so my father died, as he said, fighting. He struck down one of his foes as he fell in the heap of slain.

The end came suddenly and almost unexpectedly and with a rush. It came at night and when all was dark save when there was a gleam of light from the flash and flame of a fired gun. Our men fought hard all day long. Their ammunition was very low. That of many was entirely spent. Santa Anna must have known this, for his men had been able during the day to make several breeches in the walls. Our men had fought long and hard and well. But their strength was spent. Many slept. Few there were who were awake. Even those on guard besides the breeches in the walls dozed. The fire from the Mexicans had slacked and finally ceased. Those who were awake saw the Mexican foeman lying quietly by their camp fires and thought they likewise slept.

But our foes were only simulating sleep or if they slept, were awakened by their savage chief and his brutal officers.

After all had been dark and quiet for many hours and I had fallen into a profound slumber suddenly there was a terrible din. Cannon boomed. Their shot crashed through the doors and windows and the breeches in the walls. Then men rushed in on us. They swarmed among us and over us. They fired on us in volleys. They struck us down with their *escopetas.* In the dark our men groped and grasped the throats of our foeman and buried their knives into their hearts.

By my side was an American boy. He was about my own age but larger. As they reached us he rose to his feet. He had been sleeping, but like myself, he had been rudely awakened. As they rushed upon him he stood calmly and across his shoulders drew the blanket on which he had slept. He was unarmed. They slew him where he stood and his corpse fell over me. My father's body was lying near the cannon which he had tended. My mother with my sister was kneeling beside it. My brothers and I were close to her. I clutched her garments. Behind her crouched the only man who escaped and was permitted to surrender. His name was Brigido Guerrera.

As they rushed upon us the Mexican soldiers faltered as they saw a woman. My mother clasped her babe to her breast and closed her eyes. She expected they would kill her and her babe and me and my brothers. I thought so too. My blood ran cold and I grew faint and sick.

Brigido Guerrera pleaded for mercy. He told them he was a prisoner in the Alamo and had been brought there against his will. He said he had tried to escape and join Santa Anna's men. They spared him. They let him out, an officer going with him.

They took my mother, her babe, my brothers and I to another part of the building where there were other women and children huddled. Another of the women had a babe at her breast. This was Mrs. Dickinson. There was an old woman in there. They called her Donna Petra. This was the only name I ever knew her by. With her was a young girl, Trinidad Saucedo, who was very beautiful. Mrs. Alsberry [sic] and her sister were there also and several other women, young girls and little boys. I do not remember having seen Madam Candalaria [sic] there. She may have been there and I shall not dispute her word. I did not notice the women as closely as I did the men.

After the soldiers of Santa Anna had got in a corner all of the women and children who had not been killed in the onslaught, they kept firing on the men who had defended the Alamo. For fully a quarter of an hour they kept firing upon them after all of the defenders had been slain and their corpses were lying still. It was pitch dark in the Eastern end of the structure and the soldiers of Santa Anna seemed to fear to go there even after firing from the Constitutionalists from there had ceased. Santa Anna's men stood still and fired into the darkness and until someone brought lanterns.

The last I saw of my father's corpse was when one of them held his lantern above it and over the dead who lay about the cannon he had tended.

It has been stated that one of the women who claims to have been in the Alamo during its siege and capture, has also claimed that she brought water into the Alamo from the ditch outside. This is not true. When we got into the Alamo, which was before access to the ditch had been entirely cut off by the soldiers of Santa Anna, such occurrence had been foreseen and forestalled by inmates of the Alamo chapel. They had already sunk a well in the church and the water therefrom was then being drunk by the occupants instead of the water from the ditch. A number of cattle had also been driven into the court of the Convent. These latter furnished food for the besieged up to the day of the fall of the Alamo. I do not recollect the inmates having suffered for either food or water during the entire period of the siege. The only article that was scarce was ammunition. This got scarcer and scarcer each day, with no chance or hope of replenishing.

The old Convent had been used for barracks by Bowie, Travis, and Crockett's men and was so used until the besiegers had driven them to seek final refuge in the chapel after a number of breeches had been made in the Convent wall. Communication was constantly kept up between the Convent & the church buildings. This was done through a door connecting them. I was in the Convent several times, but stayed most, and practically all, of the time in the church, as it was considered safest. Crockett who, as I said before they called Don Benito, went into the Convent and stayed there for some time. But he was everywhere during the siege and personally slew many of the enemy with his rifle, his pistol and his knife. He fought hand to hand. He clubbed his rifle when they closed in on him and knocked them down with its stock until he was overwhelmed by numbers and slain. He fought to his last breath. He fell immediately in front of the large double doors which he defended with the force that was by his side. Crockett was one of the few who were wide awake when the final crisis and crash came. When he died there was a heap of slain in front and on each side of him. These he had all killed before he finally fell on top of the heap.

Travis spent most of his time directing the firing from the roof of the church. He too, seemed not only dauntless but sleepless. He encouraged the gunners. Whenever a good shot was made with the cannon he commended them. He told them where to aim and where to fire efficaciously, the cannon fire from the roof of the church being most of the time under his direct personal supervision. Crockett and he both, however, looked after the cannonading from the Convent as well, both making repeated visits to that locality and at frequent intervals.

Bowie, although ill and suffering from a fever, fought until he was so severely wounded that he had to be carried to his cot, which was placed in one of the smaller rooms on the north side of the church. Even after he was confined to his cot he fought, firing his pistol and, occasionally, his rifle at the enemy after the soldiers of Santa Anna had entered the church and some of them got into his room. He loaded and fired his weapons until his foes closed in on him. When they made their final rush upon him, he rose up in his bed and received them. He buried his sharp knife into the breast of one of them as another fired the shot that killed him. He was literally riddled with bullets. I saw his corpse before we were taken out of the building.

Mrs. Alsbury and my mother were among those who nursed and ministered to his wants. Mrs. Alsbury was near him when he was killed, while my mother and I were in the large main room of the church and by the cannon near the window where my father fell.

The shot and shells tore great holes in the walls. They also sawed out great jagged segments of the walls of both the Convent and the church. The roof of the Convent was knocked in, the greater part of it falling, as also did a considerable portion of the roof of the church. Nearly one-half of the walls of the Convent were knocked off. . . .

Although I do not remember to have seen any one killed in the Convent, because I was not in there when they were, I am told and believe that many of the defenders of the Alamo perished there. . . .

After all of the men had been slain, the women and children

were kept huddled up in the church's southwest corner in the small room to the right of the large double door of the church as one enters it. A guard was put over them. They were held there until after daylight when orders were given to remove them. We were all marched off to the house of Senor Musquiz. Here all of the women were again placed under guard. Musquiz owned a suerte on South Alamo Street not very far from where the Beethoven Hall now is. My mother and father were well acquainted with the Musquiz family. At about 8:00 we became very hungry, up to then not having been given any food. My mother, being familiar with the premises, began to look about for food for herself and children as well as her other comrades. While she was doing so Musquiz told her that it was dangerous for her to be moving about and leaving the place, and room in which she was under guard. She told him she did not care if she was under guard or not, she was going to have something to eat for herself, her children and her companions whom she intended to feed if Santa Anna did not feed his prisoners. Musquiz admonished her to silence and told her to be patient and he would get them some food from his own store.

After urging my mother not to leave the room, Musquiz disappeared and went to his pantry, where he got quite a quantity of provision and brought them to the room in which the prisoners, some 10 or a dozen in number, were and distributed the food among them. There was some coffee as well as bread and meat. I recollect that I ate heartily, but my mother very sparingly.

We were kept at Musquiz's house until 3:00 in the afternoon when the prisoners were taken to Military Plaza.

We were halted on the plaza and in front of the place where Wolfson's store now is. Mrs. Alsbury and her sister, Mrs. Gertrudes [*sic*] Cantu [Navarro], were the first ones to be taken before Santa Anna. He questioned them and after talking with them for a few minutes, discharged them from custody and they left. Mrs. Cantu afterwards removed to the Calaveras where she married and resided up to the time of her death.

My mother was next called before the dictator. When she appeared before him my baby sister pressed closely to her bosom, I with my brother followed her into his presence. My brother was clinging to her skirt, but I stood to one side and behind her. I watched every move and listened to every word spoken. Santa Anna asked her name. She gave it. He then asked, "Where is your husband?" She answered sobbing: "He's dead at the Alamo." Santa Anna next asked where the other members of the family were. She replied a brother of my father's, she was informed, was in his (Santa Anna's) army. This was true. My father had a brother whose name was Francisco Esparza, who joined the forces of Santa Anna. It was this brother who appeared before Santa Anna later and asked permission to search among the slain for my father's corpse. The permission was given. My uncle found my father's body and had it buried in the Campo Santo where Milam Square is now. I did not get a chance to see it before it was buried there, as the burial, as all others incident to that battle, was a very hurried one. It was probable that my father was the only one who fought on the side of the Constitutionalists, and against the force of the dictator, whose body was buried without having first been burned.

Santa Anna released my mother. He gave her a blanket and two silver dollars as he dismissed her. I was informed that he gave a blanket and the same sum of money to each of the other women who were brought from the Alamo before him.

I noticed him closely and saw he was the same officer I had seen dismount on the Main Plaza about sundown of the night when I went into the Alamo. After our release we went back to our home and my mother wept for many days and nights. I frequently went to the Main Plaza and watched the soldiers of Santa Anna and saw him quite a number of times before they marched away towards Houston where he [Santa Anna] was defeated. He had a very broad face and high cheek bones. He had a hard and cruel look and his countenance was a very sinister one. It has haunted me ever since I last saw it and I will never forget the face or figure of Santa Anna.

# Hanging Around the Alamo

## Bryan Woolley

I WAS hanging around the Alamo the other day, looking at the tourists.

Tourists are much the same everywhere, I guess. Most dress in clothes they wouldn't wear in their own hometowns, except maybe in their backyards. They all strike the same poses for whoever's holding the Instamatic, and most of them spend more time in the curio shop, buying souvenirs made in Taiwan and Hong Kong, than looking at the sight they came to see.

Alamo tourists are like that. They're a little disappointed in what they're looking at, I think. The Alamo is so small and unprepossessing, as historic shrines go, that it can't live up to its billing.

And its story, as told in the exhibits inside, requires more reading than most tourists have time or patience for. Unless they've paid their money to see the multiscreen slide presentation at the Remember the Alamo Museum across the plaza, most don't know that the remaining structure was only a small part of the original fortress, and that many of the heroes fell in what is now the lobby of the U.S. Post Office and in the street where the taxicabs are honking and along the line of cheap stores across the way.

Although some have seen John Wayne's movie and know that his Davy Crockett and the rest died for "freedom," not many know what complaints the Texas settlers had against the Mexican government that could have led to such bloody results. Most don't really care. The Alamo is just one of those things it's nice to have seen, like Mount Vernon or Independence Hall, but not as interesting to look at.

Maybe I would have felt the same as they do if I hadn't learned the Alamo's story at my grandmother's knee when I was five years old. It was the first time I heard of William Travis's famous line—how on March 4, 1836, after ten days of siege and all hope of help had flown, the Alamo commander gathered his men and told them of their approaching doom if they remained; how he drew his sword and traced a long line in the dirt and said, "I now want every man who is determined to stay here and die with me to come across this line. Who will be the first?"

And as she told of those men stepping one by one over the line, of ailing Jim Bowie asking his comrades to lift his cot across, leaving cowardly Moses Rose standing alone, my small chest filled with that pride of heritage that makes Texans so obnoxious to the rest of the world.

I've been an Alamo nut ever since. I've read dozens of accounts of the siege. I know its history has been interlaced with legend and fantasy and speculation and that grandmothers and textbooks and movies often draw our heroes more heroic than they really were.

I've learned that the battle took place during the Romantic Age, when men everywhere were making noble speeches and fighting revolutions, and that it was more fashionable in those days to die for glory than it is now. I've learned that the Alamo's most famous heroes—William Travis, Jim Bowie, Jim Bonham, and Davy Crockett—were rascals of the first order, firebrand adventurers with plenty of past to live down. If they hadn't been such spellbinders, maybe the more ordinary men in their command wouldn't have rushed so willingly to their own much smaller measures of immortality.

But all that matters not a whit to me. My knowledge of my heroes' weaknesses has made them only dearer to me, their ghosts more accessible, easier to commune with than the noble, strong faces in the shrine's idealized paintings.

So every time I'm in San Antonio, I do my Alamo ritual, studying the familiar relics and paintings, reading Travis's passionate, futile appeals for help: "To the people of Texas and all Americans in the world—Fellow citizens—& compatriots—I am besieged by a thousand or more of the Mexicans under Santa Anna . . . *I shall never surrender or retreat.* Then, I call on you in the name of Liberty, of patriotism & everything dear to the American character, to come to our aid and with all dispatch, . . ."

The ghosts were particularly active the day I was there, the 143rd anniversary of Travis's last speech to his men—"I have deceived you by the promise of help. . . ."—and his line in the dirt. The names of the dead on the bronze plaques on the old stone walls seemed more vivid than before, each seeming to call attention to itself: Tapley Holland, Ohio (the first to cross the line); Micajah Autry, North Carolina; Daniel William Cloud, Kentucky; Robert W. Ballentine, Scotland; Asa Walker, Tennessee; Charles Zanco, Denmark. Only a handful of the defenders were born in Texas, I noticed, and nearly all with Spanish names:

Abamillo, Badillo, Esparza, Fuentes, Guerrero, Losoya. And I haven't yet found the plaque of one name on the Alamo's list of heroes: John, Negro.

But their birthplaces don't matter much to history, and neither do the lives of most of them. Some had lived in Texas for years; others arrived just in time to die and become part of a legend, a mystique, a heritage—whatever it is that makes the Alamo the center of the Texan soul as surely as the Temple in Jerusalem is the center of the Jewish soul.

Maybe that's what makes the Alamo disappointing as a tourist attraction. The Instamatic can't capture soul, and the Taiwanese haven't quite duplicated it. The closest they've come is a synthetic coonskin cap and a plastic rifle.

What the Alamo needs, I think, is my grandmother. "Thermopylae had its messenger of defeat," she would tell the sightseers. "The Alamo had none."

They might wonder what the hell Thermopylae is, but their hearts would be moved.

# The Sense of Place

## Rolando Hinojosa

I BEGIN with a quote from a man imprisoned for his participation in the Texas-Santa Fe Expedition of 1841; while in his
cell in Mexico City, he spurned Santa Anna's offer of freedom in
exchange for renouncing the Republic of Texas. Those words of
1842 were said by a man who had signed the Texas Declaration
of Independence and who had served in the Congress of the Republic. Later on, he was to cast a delegate vote for annexation
and contributed to the writing of the first state constitution. He
would win election to the state legislature and still later he
would support secession.

And this is what he said: "I have sworn to be a good Texan;
and that I will not forswear. I will die for that which I firmly believe, for I know it is just and right. One life is a small price for a
cause so great. As I fought, so shall I be willing to die. I will
never forsake Texas and her cause. I am her son."

The words were written by José Antonio Navarro. A Texas
historian named James Wilson once wrote that Navarro's name
is virtually unknown to Texas school children and, for the most
part, unknown to their teachers as well. A lifetime of living in
my native land leads me to believe that Professor Wilson is cor-
rect in his assessment of the lack of knowledge of this place in
which we were born and in which some of us still live.

The year 1983 marks the one hundredth anniversary of the
birth of my father, Manuel Guzmán Hinojosa, in the Campacuás
Ranch, some three miles north of Mercedes, down in the Valley;
his father was born on that ranch as was his father's father. On
the maternal side, my mother arrived in the Valley at the age of
six-weeks in the year 1887 along with one of the first Anglo-
American settlers enticed to the mid-Valley by Jim Wells, one of
the early developers on the northern bank. As you may already
know, it's no accident that Jim Wells County in South Texas is
named for him.

One of the earliest stories I heard about Grandfather Smith
was a supposed conversation he held with Lawyer Wells. You are
being asked to imagine the month of July in the Valley with no air
conditioning in 1887; Wells was extolling the Valley and he said
that all it needed was a little water and a few good people. My

grandfather replied, "Well, that's all Hell needs, too." The story is apocryphal; it has to be. But living in the Valley, and hearing that type of story laid the foundation for what I later learned was to give me a sense of place. By that I do not mean that I had a feel for the place; no, not at all. I had a sense of it, and by that I mean that I was not learning about the culture of the Valley, but living it, forming part of it, and thus, contributing to it.

But a place is merely that until it is populated, and once populated, the histories of the place and its people begin. For me and mine, history began in 1749 when the first colonists began moving into the southern and northern banks of the Río Grande. That river was not yet a jurisdictional barrier and was not to be until almost one hundred years later; but, by then, the border had its own history, its own culture, and its own sense of place: it was Nuevo Santander, named for old Santander in the Spanish Peninsula.

The last names were similar up and down on both banks of the river, and as second and third cousins were allowed to marry, this further promulgated and propagated blood relationships and that sense of belonging that led the Borderers to label their fellow Mexicans who came from the interior, as *fuereños*, or outsiders; and later, when the people from the North started coming to the Border, these were labeled *gringos*, a word for foreigner, and nothing else, until the *gringo* himself, from all evidence, took the term as a pejorative label.

For me, then, part of a sense of the Border came from sharing: the sharing of names, of places, of a common history, and of belonging to the place; one attended funerals, was taken to cemeteries, and one saw names that corresponded to one's own or to one's friends and neighbors, and relatives.

When I first started to write, and being what we call "empapado," which translates as drenched, imbibed, soaked, or drunk with the place, I had to eschew the romanticism and the sentimentalism that tend to blind the unwary, that get in the way of truth. It's no great revelation when I say that romanticism and sentimentalism tend to corrupt clear thinking as well. The Border wasn't paradise, and it didn't have to be; but it was more than paradise, it was home (and as Frost once wrote, home, when you have to go there, is the place where they have to take you in).

And the Border was home; and it was also the home of the petty officeholder elected by an uninformed citizenry; a home for bossism, and for old-time smuggling as a way of life for some.

But, it also maintained the remains of a social democracy that cried out for independence, for a desire to be left alone, and for the continuance of a sense of community.

The history one learned there was an oral one and somewhat akin to the oral religion brought by the original colonials. Many of my generation were raised with the music written and composed by Valley people, and we learned the ballads of the Border little knowing that it was a true native art form. And one was also raised and steeped in the stories and exploits of Juan Nepomuceno Cortina, in the nineteenth century, and with stories of the Texas Rangers in that century and of other Ranger stories in this century and then, as always, names, familiar patronymics: Jacinto Treviño, Aniceto Pizaña, the Seditionists of 1915 who had camped in Mercedes, and where my father would take me and show and mark for me the spot where the Seditionists had camped and barbecued their meat half a generation before. These were men of flesh and bone who lived and died there in Mercedes, in the Valley. And then there were the stories of the Revolution of 1910, and of the participation in it for the next ten years off and on by Valley *mexicanos* who fought alongside their south bank relatives, and the stories told to me and to those of my generation by exiles, men and women from Mexico, who earned a living by teaching us school on the northern bank while they bided their time to return to Mexico.

But we didn't return to Mexico; we didn't have to; we were Borderers with a living and unifying culture born of conflict with another culture and this, too, helped to cement further still the knowing exactly where one came from and from whom one was descended.

The language, too, was a unifier and as strong an element as there is in fixing one's sense of place; the language of the Border is a derivative of the Spanish language of Northern Mexico, a language wherein some nouns and other grammatical complements were no longer used in the Spanish Peninsula, but which persisted there; and the more the linguistically uninformed went out of their way to denigrate the language, the stiffer the resistance to maintain it and to nurture it on the northern bank. And the uninformed failed, of course, for theirs was a momentary diversion while one was committed to its preservation; the price that many Texas Mexicans paid for keeping the language and the sense of place has been exorbitant.

As Borderers, the northbank Border Mexican couldn't, to repeat a popular phrase, "go back to where you came from." The

Borderer was there and had been before the interlopers; but what of the indigenous population prior to the 1749 settlement? Since Nuevo Santander was never under the presidio system and since its citizens did not build missions that trapped and stultified the indigenous people, they remained there and, in time, settled down or were absorbed by the colonial population and thus the phrase hurled at the Border Mexican "go back to where you came from" was, to use another popular term, "inoperative." And this, too, fostered that sense of place.

For the writer—this writer—a sense of place was not a matter of importance; it became essential. And so much so that my stories are not held together by the *peripeteia* or the plot as much as by *what* the people who populate the stories say and *how* they say it, how they look at the world out and the world in; and the works, then, become studies of perceptions and values and decisions reached by them because of those perceptions and values which in turn were fashioned and forged by the place and its history.

What I am saying here is not to be taken to mean that it is impossible for a writer to write about a place, its history, and its people, if the writer is not from that particular place; it can be done, and it has been done. What I *am* saying is that I needed a sense of place, and that this helped me no end in the way that, I would say, Américo Paredes in *With His Pistol in His Hand,* McMurtry in *Horseman, Pass By* and Gipson in *Hound Dog Man,* and Owens in that fine, strong *This Stubborn Soil,* and Tomás Rivera in . . . *and the earth did not part* were all helped by a sense of place. And I say this, because to me, these writers and others impart a sense of place and a sense of truth about the place and about the values of that place. It isn't a studied attitude, but rather one of a certain love, to use that phrase, and an understanding for the place that they captured in print for themselves; something that was, for themselves, then, at that time and there. A sense of place, as Newark, New Jersey, is for Phillip Roth, and thus we see him surprised at himself when he tells us he dates a *schicksa,* and then, the wonderful storyteller that he is, he tells us of his Jewish traditions and conflicts, and we note that it becomes a pattern in some of his writings whenever he writes of relationships, which, after all, is what writers usually write about: relationships.

I am not making a medieval pitch for the shoemaker to stick to his last here, but if the writer places a lifetime of living in a work, the writer sometimes finds it difficult to remove the place of provenance from the writings, irrespective of where he situates his stories. That's a strong statement and one which may elicit comment or disagreement, but what spine one has is formed early in life, and it is formed at a specific place; later on when one grows up, one may mythicize, adopt a persona, become an actor, restructure family history, but the original facts of one's formation remain as facts always do.

It's clear, then, that I am not speaking of the formula novel, nor is it my intent to denigrate it or its practitioners; far from it. I consider the formula novel as a fine art, if done well, and many of us know that they do exist. I speak of something else—neither nobler nor better, no—merely different from that genre. It's a personal thing, because I found that after many years of hesitancy, and fits and spurts, and false starts, that despite what education I had acquired, I was still limited in many ways; that whatever I attempted to write, came out false and frail. Now, I know I wanted to write, had to write, was burning to write and all of those things that some writers say to some garden clubs, but the truth and heart of the matter was that I did not know where to begin; and there it was again, that adverb of place, the *where;* and then I got lucky: I decided to write whatever it was I had, in Spanish, and I decided to set it on the border, in the Valley. As reduced as that space was, it too was Texas with all of its contradictions and its often repeated one-sided telling of Texas history. When the characters stayed in the Spanish-speaking milieu or society, the Spanish language worked well, and then it was in the natural order of things that English made its entrance when the characters strayed or found themselves in Anglo institutions; in cases where both cultures would come into contact, both languages were used, and I would employ both, and where one and only one would do, I would follow that as well; what dominated, then, was the place, at first. Later on I discovered that generational and class differences also dictated not only usage but which language as well. From this came the *how* they said *what* they said. As the census rolls filled up in the works, so did some distinguishing features, characteristics, viewpoints, values, decisions, and thus I used the Valley and the Border, and the history and the people. The freedom to do this also led me to use the folklore and the anthropology of the Valley and to use whatever literary form I desired and saw fit to use to tell my stories: dialogs, duologs, monologs, imaginary newspaper clippings, and whatever else I felt would be of use. And it *was* the Valley, but it remained forever Texas. At the same time, I could see this Valley, this border, and I drew a map, and this, too, was another key, and this led to more work and to more characters in that place.

It was a matter of luck in some ways, as I said, but mostly it was the proper historical moment; it came along, and I took what had been there for some time, but which I had not been able to see, since I had not fully developed a sense of place; I had left the Valley for the service, for formal university training, and for a series of very odd jobs, only to return to it in my writing.

I have mentioned values and decisions; as I see them, these are matters inculcated by one's elders first, by one's acquaintances later on, and usually under the influence of one's society which is another way of saying one's place of origin. Genetic structure may enter into holding to certain values and perhaps in the manner of reaching decisions, for all I know. Ortega y Gasset, among others, I suspect, wrote that man makes dozens of decisions every day, and that the process helps man to make and to reach more serious, deliberate, and even important decisions when the time presents itself. A preparatory stage, as it were. The point of this is that my decision to write what I write and where I choose to situate the writing is not based on anything else other than to write about what I know, the place I know, the language used, the values held. When someone mentions universality, I say that what happens to my characters happens to other peoples of the world at given times, and I've no doubt on that score. What has helped me to write has also been a certain amount of questionable self-education, a long and fairly misspent youth in the eyes of some, an acceptance of certain facts and some misrepresentations of the past which I could not change, but which led to a rejection not of those unalterable facts but of hypocrisy and the smugness of the self-satisfied. For this and other personal reasons, humor creeps into my writing once in a while, because it was the use of irony, as many of us know, that allowed the Borderer to survive and to maintain a certain measure of dignity.

Serious writing is deliberate as well as a consequence of an arrived-to decision; what one does with it may be of value or not, but I believe that one's fidelity to history is the first step in fixing a sense of place, whether that place is a worldwide arena or a corner of it, as is mine.

# "And the Skies Are Not Cloudy All Day"

## Alan Bosworth

*Popular culture suggests the Colt revolver tamed the West. In fact it was barbed wire and the windmill. The following is from Ozona County, by Alan Bosworth. Ironically, tiny Ozona became the richest, by per capita income, town in America when the drillers went a little deeper and opened the Ozona oilfield.*

SEPTEMBER rain means greened-up pastures, and juicy calf ribs in the spring. But Ozona ranchmen were not long in discovering that many a September is hot and dry, that the annual precipitation in Crockett County averages just a fraction over sixteen inches, and that it is a long way to water in any direction—especially down. The first comers were quick to acquire the few dependable waterholes, such as Howard's Well and Escondido—both historic overnight camping places on the old San Antonio-Chihuahua Trail. The whole land is tilted southwestward, and water runs off it with flash-flood speed. What stayed behind, in Gurley or Johnson Draws, was soon "too thick to swallow and too thin to chew," and cowboys forced to drink out of cowtracks in the mud quickly developed the habit of straining the water through their teeth. They could have understood the wariness of the late Gene Fowler, who all his life would never drink to the bottom of any glass because, when he was a boy in the Rockies, "there was always some sort of a bug surprise at the bottom."

Well drillers and windmills saved the day, and the nineties in the Ozona country might well be called the Windmill Era. It seems rather strange and a little sad that no literature has ever really given the well driller and the windmill man their due. I do not know of a man of either breed who ever got rich, although they helped others to riches. The drillers were a peripatetic sort, always moving westward with the frontier; they might be compared with Johnny Appleseed, on an earlier and more fruitful border. Some of the windmill men stayed, or grew up to practice their trade . . . usually one or two to an entire county. But the time came when a single large ranch had a half dozen or more windmills and could afford to hire its own full-time windmill man. Cowboys were sometimes forced to learn a new skill.

A ranch hand might curse the windmill for its rhythmic creaking and rattling at night, but it was not long before this became a sort of lullaby, and if the noise suddenly stopped due to a breakdown he would sit upright in his bed tarp, knowing that about sunup he would have to be up on the platform, perhaps in a freezing wind, trying to fix the dadblamed thing. Until later models came out with a self-oiling device, windmills had to be greased at appallingly short intervals, and you could always tell a windmill man from afar by the spatter of oil that inevitably dripped on his hat and jumper when he went back down the ladder after finishing a greasing job. Still, there was pride in being an all-around ranch hand. . . .

The well Joe Moore drilled in 1885, on land that later became Judge Charles E. Davidson's ranch, seems to have been the first; the E. M. Powell well on the Ozona townsite probably was the second, but from then on through the turn of the century and for long afterward well drillers were exceedingly active. Some used steam drills; others had rigs powered by horses walking in a circle, with water that had to be hauled a long way being poured into the hole at intervals to soften the earth and hasten the progress. Some wells struck "blue mud"—a sure sign, in those days, of a "dry hole"—and the rig would be moved to a new location. The depth might be a hundred feet, two hundred, or four hundred, before the long bailing bucket with a valve in its bottom brought up water. When this sloshed out on the trampled grass, the liquid sound was music, the sight was answer to a prayer.

Having struck water, the ranch owner would then either take his own wagons to the Findlater Hardware Company or another dealer in San Angelo, or would order his windmill and pipe brought down by a freighter. Almost invariably, the tail fans bore the brand names of Eclipse, Sampson, or Aermotor. The Eclipse had a huge, slatted wooden wheel and tail fin, and required a considerable breeze. It would, in the memory of ranchman Ernest Dunlap, "bring up water with every turn of that big wheel—and then not run again until next March." But whatever brand it was, the new windmill worked its magic deep in the earth, day and night, to bring a thin stream of bright water fluting from the lead pipe and splashing into some sort of storage reservoir—a dirt tank scraped out of the ground, a circular stone and cement tank, or a taller one made of galvanized iron.

The perhaps apocryphal cowboy who swore he could drink water faster than the new mill could pump it was talking through his Stetson: given time, with the incessant wind, and the tank would be brimming over.

There was no assurance of getting *good* water. Old-timers insisted that the Pecos River was so alkaline a kildee only had to fly across it to get the diarrhea, and the subterranean water was often even more strongly mineral—usually sulphurous. Ranchmen theorized that sulphur water most often came from wells drilled in the mesquite flats. Besides, a windmill on a divide or hillpoint got more breeze. But many of these pumped sulphur water too—some of it smelling uncomfortably like rotten eggs. Nobody ever bothered to bottle this for medicinal use, although not far away on the South Concho River near Christoval, a health resort was springing up around a series of sulphur springs, and small boys who swam in ranch tanks found that sulphur water very quickly healed skinned shins and stubbed toes.

The George Harrell ranch south of Ozona had only sulphur water for a long time. It made wretched coffee, shriveled the *frijole* beans, and formed black sediment in the pipes and troughs. Then Mr. Harrell's only son, R. A. (Alvin), went off to the University of Texas and came back with a degree.

Mr. Harrell, a progressive man, was eager for his son to take over and put his learning to work along scientific lines. There were advancements in livestock breeding, in range management, and in drenching sheep for stomach worms. He asked Alvin what was the first thing he intended to do.

After one is around sulphur water for a time one becomes accustomed to both the taste and the smell. But Alvin was newly home from Austin. He sniffed downwind from the well, and said, "I'm going to do something about this water!"

Mr. Harrell stepped back and waited for geological surveys and other scientific tests. There was none. Instead, Alvin went to Ozona and arranged for Tom Smith to "witch" for water with a pronged willow switch.

Tom Smith—an unlikely name for a necromancer—had been blacksmith and constable in Ozona from the earliest days. A very powerful man physically, he never carried a gun, and he set something of a record by never making an arrest. (This, much later, got him featured in Robert L. Ripley's *Believe It or Not.*) He simply heaved troublemakers out of public places and sent them home.

Now he walked across the mesquite flat at the Harrell ranch with the willow fork held before him at chest level, something like a man walking in his sleep. George Harrell followed, shaking his head dubiously.

They went a long way through the tangled chaparral. About a mile from the ranch house, the willow dipped sharply in Tom's grasp. He scratched a mark on the hard ground with his boot heel, and said, "Drill right here."

They drilled, and struck abundant water, cold and sweet, which still supplies the ranch house and the stock in that pasture.

Mr. Harrell told the story for a long time. It plainly showed, he said, the advantages of a college education.

*from*

# The Mountain Chant

## (Navajo)

### First Song of the Thunder

Thonah! Thonah!
There is a voice above,
The voice of the thunder.
Within the dark cloud,
Again and again it sounds,
Thonah! Thonah!

Thonah! Thonah!
There is a voice below;
The voice of the grasshopper.
Among the plants,
Again and again it sounds,
Thonah! Thonah!

### Twelfth Song of the Thunder

The voice that beautifies the land!
The voice above,
The voice of the thunder
Within the dark cloud
Again and again it sounds,
The voice that beautifies the land.

The voice that beautifies the land!
The voice below,
The voice of the grasshopper
Among the plants
Again and again it sounds,
The voice that beautifies the land.

# You Have to Be Careful

## Naomi Shihab Nye

You have to be careful telling things.
Some ears are tunnels.
Your words will go in and get lost in the dark.
Some ears are flat pans like the miners used
looking for gold.
What you say will be washed out with the stones.

You look a long time till you find the right ears.
Till then, there are birds and lamps to be spoken to,
a patient cloth rubbing shine in circles,
and the slow, gradual growing possibility
that when you find such ears,
they already know.

# My Father and the Figtree

## Naomi Shihab Nye

For other fruits my father was indifferent.
He'd point at the cherry trees and say,
"See those? I wish they were figs."
In the evenings he sat by my bed
weaving folktales like vivid little scarves.
They always involved a figtree.
Even when it didn't fit, he'd stick it in.
Once Joha was walking down the road
and he saw a figtree.
Or, he tied his camel to a figtree
and went to sleep.
Or, later when they caught and arrested him,
his pockets were full of figs.

At age six I ate a dried fig and shrugged.
"That's not what I'm talking about!" he said.
"I'm talking about a fig straight from the earth—
gift of Allah!—on a branch so heavy it touches the ground.
I'm talking about picking the largest fattest sweetest fig
in the world and putting it in my mouth."
(Here he'd stop and close his eyes.)

Years passed, we lived in many houses, none had figtrees.
We had lima beans, zucchini, parsley, beets.
"Plant one!" my mother said, but my father never did.
He tended garden half-heartedly, forgot to water,
let the okra get too big.
"What a dreamer he is. Look how many things he starts
and doesn't finish."

The last time he moved, I had a phone call,
my father, in Arabic, chanting a song I'd never heard.
"What's that?"
"Wait till you see!"

He took me out to the new yard.
There, in the middle of Dallas, Texas,
a tree with the largest, fattest, sweetest figs in the world.
"It's a figtree song!" he said,
plucking his fruits like ripe tokens,
emblems, assurance
of a world that was always his own.

# I Am Singing Now

## Luci Tapahonso

the moon is a white sliver
balancing the last of its contents
in the final curve of the month
my daughters sleep
in the back of the pickup
breathing small clouds of white in the dark
they lie warm and soft
under layers of clothes and blankets
how they dream, precious ones, of grandma
and the scent of fire
the smell of mutton
they are already home.

i watch the miles dissolve behind us
in the hazy glow of taillights and
the distinct shape of hills and mesas loom above
then recede slowly in the clear winter night.

i sing to myself and
think of my father
teaching me, leaning towards me
listening as i learned.
"just like this," he would say
and he would sing those old songs

into the fiber of my hair,
into the pores of my skin,
into the dreams of my children

and i am singing now
for the night
the almost empty moon
and the land swimming beneath cold bright stars.

# Señora X No More

## Pat Mora

Straight as a nun I sit.
My fingers foolish before paper and pen
hide in my palms. I hear the slow, accented echo
     How are yu? I ahm fine. How are yu?
of the other women who clutch notebooks
and blush at their stiff lips resisting
sounds that float gracefully as
bubbles from their children's mouths.
My teacher bends over me, gently squeezes
my shoulders, the squeeze I give my sons,
hands louder than words.
She slides her arms around me:
a warm shawl, lifts my left arm
onto the cold, lined paper.
"*Señora*, don't let it slip away," she says
and opens the ugly, soap-wrinkled fingers
of my right hand with a pen like I pry open
the lips of a stubborn grandchild.
My hand cramps around the thin hardness.
"Let it breathe," says this woman who knows
my hand and tongue knot, but she guides
and I dig the tip of my pen into that white.
I carve my crooked name, and again at night
until my hand and arm are sore,
I carve my crooked name,
my name.

# Haciendo Apenas
# la Recolección

## Tino Villanueva

For weeks now
I have not been able
to liberate me from my name.
Always I am history I must wake to.
In idiot defeat I trace my routes
across a half-forgotten map of Texas.
I smooth out the folds stubborn
as the memory.

Let me see: I would start from San Marcos,
moving northward,
bored beyond recognition
in the stale air of a '52 Chevy:
to my left, the youngest of uncles
steadies the car;
to my right, grandfather finds humor
in the same joke.
I am hauled among family
extended across the back seat,
as the towns bury themselves forever
in my eyes:   Austin, Lampasas, Brownwood,
past Abilene, Sweetwater,
along
the Panhandle's alien tallness.
There it is:   Lubbock sounding harsh as ever.
I press its dark letters,
and dust on my fingertips is so alive
it startles them
as once did sand.
Then west, 10,000 acres and a finger's breadth,
is Levelland,
where a thin house once stood,
keeping watch over me and my baseball glove
when the wrath of winds cleared the earth

of stooping folk.
There's Ropesville, where in fifth grade
I didn't make a friend.

My arm is taut by now and terrified.
It slackens,
begins falling back into place
while the years are gathering slowly
along still roads and hill country,
downward
to where it all began—500 McKie Street.
I am home, and although the stars
are at rest tonight,
my strength is flowing.

Weep no more, my common hands;
you shall not again
pick cotton.

# Love Poem

## Leslie Marmon Silko

Rain smell comes with the wind
                      out of the southwest.
Smell of the sand dunes
             tall grass glistening
                        in the rain.
Warm raindrops that fall easy
                (this woman)
The summer is born.
Smell of her breathing new life
              small gray toads on damp sand.
(this woman)
         whispering to dark wide leaves
         white moon blossoms dripping
                  tracks in the sand.
Rain smell
         I am full of hunger
         deep and longing to touch
wet tall grass, green and strong beneath.
This woman loved a man
and she breathed to him
             her damp earth song.
I am haunted by this story
I remember it in cottonwood leaves
               their fragrance in the shade.
I remember it in the wide blue sky
when the rain smell comes with the wind.

# A Story of How a Wall Stands

## Simon Ortiz

*At Aacqu, there is a wall almost 400 years old which sup-
ports hundreds of tons of dirt and bones—it's a graveyard
built on a steep incline—and it looks like it's about to fall
down the incline but will not for a long time.*

My father, who works with stone,
says, "That's just the part you see,
the stones which seem to be
just packed in on the outside,"
and with his hands puts the stone and mud
in place. "Underneath what looks like loose stone,
there is stone woven together."
He ties one hand over the other,
fitting like the bones of his hands
and fingers. "That's what is
holding it together."

"It is built that carefully,"
he says, "the mud mixed
to a certain texture," patiently
"with the fingers," worked
in the palm of the hand. "So that
placed between the stones, they hold
together for a long, long time."

He tells me those things,
the story of them worked
with his fingers, in the palm
of his hands, working the stone
and the mud until they become
the wall that stands a long, long time.

# Rug of Woven Magic

## Nan Benally

I remember
  you weaving your beautiful rug
    by the kerosene lamp.

Your hands
  deftly moved
    among the strands
  mystically creating
    a design that slowly evolved
      with each row.

Sometimes I would come
  to visit
    while you were gathering
  those special herbs
that transformed each skein of
  carefully carded wool into
    hues that only nature provides.

Patiently
  you would answer my questions
  "What plants are they?",
    "Where do they come from?",
      "What are their names in English?",
             ". . . in Navaho?"

I envied your knowledge
    of all that was mysterious
      to me.
You were the
  magician that created
    rugs so beautiful from
      seemingly very little.

Your weaving
    spoke a language of its own
        that needed no interpretation.
All the magic,
    all the beauty
had already been transformed
            through you.

There are many legends
        that you have told me
            (as you sat at the loom)
        of how things came to be.
As I listened
    the rug seemed to take in
        all that you spoke.
You become a part of
        what you made,
            for in it was
    your beauty,
        your wisdom,
            your pride.

# Remember

## Joy Harjo

Remember the sky that you were born under,
know each of the star's stories.
Remember the moon, know who she is.
Remember the sun's birth at dawn, that is the
strongest point of time. Remember sundown
and the giving away to night.
Remember your birth, how your mother struggled
to give you form and breath. You are evidence of
her life, and her mother's, and hers.
Remember your father. He is your life, also.
Remember the earth whose skin you are:
red earth, black earth, yellow earth, white earth
brown earth, we are earth.
Remember the plants, trees, animal life who all have their
tribes, their families, their histories, too. Talk to them,
listen to them. They are alive poems.
Remember the wind. Remember her voice. She knows the
origin of this universe.
Remember that you are all people and that all people
are you.
Remember that you are this universe and that this
universe is you.
Remember that all is in motion, is growing, is you.
Remember that language comes from this.
Remember the dance that language is, that life is.
Remember.

# Biographical Notes

**Rudolfo A. Anaya** (born 1937) A strong interest in history infuses much of Rudolfo Anaya's writing. His first novel, *Bless Me, Ultima* (1972), won national acclaim for its moving depiction of the culture and history of New Mexico. More recently, Anaya worked with José Griego y Maestas to bring the Latino heritage to a larger audience by retelling Spanish *cuentos*, or folk tales, in English.

**T. B. Thorpe** (1815–1878) Although he was born in Massachusetts, T. B. Thorpe spent most of his life as a frontiersman. After serving in the Mexican War, Thorpe decided to become a writer. He produced many books and pamphlets about the war, as well as an assortment of "yarns," or tall tales, the most famous of which is "The Big Bear of Arkansas."

**Katherine Anne Porter** (1890–1980) Born in Indian Creek, Texas, Katherine Anne Porter began writing at an early age. As a young adult, she worked as a journalist and lived for eight years in Mexico, where a number of her stories take place. A highly acclaimed writer, Porter won the Pulitzer Prize and the National Book Award for *Collected Stories* (1965). In addition, *Ship of Fools* (1962), her novel, was made into a popular film.

**Robert Flynn** (born 1932) A writer of short stories and novels, Robert Flynn is the novelist-in-residence at Trinity University in San Antonio, Texas. His work has garnered him several awards, most recently the Spur Award from Western Writers of America and a Western Heritage Award from the National Cowboy Hall of Fame.

**Sandra Cisneros** (born 1954) Growing up in a large Mexican American family in Chicago, Sandra Cisneros spent a lot of her time reading fairy tales and classic works of literature. Her love of reading developed into a desire to write, and after college, she enrolled at the Writer's Workshop at the University of Iowa. In 1984, Cisneros published her first book, *The House on Mango Street*, a group of connected stories based on her childhood. That book, along with her more recently published stories, essays, and poems, won Cisneros acclaim as an eloquent voice in contemporary literature.

**Tomás Rivera** (1935–1984) Born in Crystal City, Texas, Tomás Rivera worked from a young age as a migrant farmer, traveling throughout the farmlands of the United States. Faced with the challenge of alternating schooling with work in the fields, Rivera pursued his education tirelessly. His persistence paid off, and he eventually earned a Ph.D. in Spanish literature and became one of the most renowned Mexican American authors in the United States.

**Luci Tapahonso** (born 1953) Like the characters in her story "The Snakeman," Diné writer Luci Tapahonso attended boarding school as a child. The story borrows from her own experiences, as well as from the traditions of the Diné (the Navajos' name for themselves). Tapahonso, a writer of both fiction and poetry, was born in Shiprock, New Mexico. In college, she met writer Leslie Marmon Silko, who encouraged Tapahonso's writing efforts. Her first book of poetry was published in 1981.

**Larry McMurtry** (born 1936) A descendant of Texas cattle ranchers, Larry McMurtry has written many exciting and humorous novels about the American West. *Lonesome Dove*, which won a Pulitzer Prize in 1986, inspired a popular television miniseries.

**Susan Shelby Magoffin** (1827–?) In the spring of 1846, nineteen-year-old Susan Shelby Magoffin became one of the first women to travel the Santa Fe Trail from Missouri to New Mexico. During the long and difficult trip, she kept a daily journal, which was published in 1926.

**Bill Groneman** (born 1952) A lifelong interest in the battle of the Alamo is evident in the work of Bill Groneman, who has published several books and articles on this single subject. This historian and writer is a member of the Alamo Society and the Texas State Historical Association.

**Bryan Woolley** (born 1937) A native of Gorman, Texas, Bryan Woolley has worked as a teacher, a journalist, and a novelist. His novel *November 22*, about the events in Dallas on the day President John F. Kennedy was assassinated, was praised by *Texas Monthly* magazine as an outstanding book about Texas. In addition to publishing works of both fiction and nonfiction, Woolley has worked as a staff writer for *The Dallas Morning News*.

**Rolando Hinojosa** (born 1929) A writer with family ties on both sides of the Texas-Mexico border, Rolando Hinojosa has published fiction in both Spanish and English. His novels, which are always set in the lower Rio Grande valley, have won him numerous awards, including the prestigious international literary prize Premio Casa de las Americas.

**Alan Bosworth** (1901–1986) A Texas native, Alan Bosworth enjoyed a long writing career that included many years as a newspaper reporter. In addition to articles such as "And the Skies Are Not Cloudy All Day," Bosworth published hundreds of short stories.

**Naomi Shihab Nye** (born 1952) This renowned poet spent her teenage years in Jerusalem and has since worked as a visiting writer at several institutions, including the University of Texas. Her books of poems have received awards, such as the Pushcart Prize, and recognition by the American Library Association.

**Pat Mora** (born 1942) Born and raised in El Paso, Texas, near the Texas-Mexico border, Pat Mora is a writer whose work depicts her appreciation of her cultural heritage, as well as the harmony she sees between Mexico and the United States. She has taught at various high schools and universities.

**Tino Villanueva** (born 1941) This Texas native has written three books of poetry, the most recent of which is *Scenes From the Movie "Giant."* His poems have also been widely anthologized.

**Leslie Marmon Silko** (born 1948) Raised on the Laguna Pueblo reservation in New Mexico, Leslie Marmon Silko grew up listening to tribal stories told by her great-grandmother and great-aunts. Drawing upon elements from the traditional tales she heard as a child, she has forged a successful career as a writer. In her stories, novels, and poems, Silko explores what life is like for Native Americans in today's world.

**Simon Ortiz** (born 1941) A writer of poetry, essays, and fiction, Simon Ortiz was born and raised in Acoma Pueblo in New Mexico. In his writing, Ortiz reveals his concern for the preservation of Native American culture and explores the relationship of all people to the land.

**Joy Harjo** (born 1951) The influence of Joy Harjo's Creek (or Muscogee) and Cherokee heritage is evident in her writing. A former member of a Native American dance troupe, Harjo attended the Institute of American Indian Arts, the University of New Mexico, and the Writer's Workshop of the University of Iowa. In addition to publishing books of poetry and prose, Harjo has also written film scripts.

# Acknowledgments *(continued from p. ii)*

**Naomi Shihab Nye**

"My Father and the Figtree" from *Different Ways to Pray* by Naomi Shihab Nye (Greitenbush Books, 1980), Copyright © 1980 by Naomi Shihab Nye. "You Have To Be Careful" from *Golden Glove* by Naomi Shihab Nye, Copyright © 1986 by Naomi Shihab Nye (Greitenbush Books). Reprinted by permission of the author.

**Simon J. Ortiz**

"A Story of How a Wall Stands" by Simon J. Ortiz from *Woven Stone*, University of Arizona Press, Tucson, AZ, 1992. Reprinted by permission of the author.

**Republic of Texas Press, an imprint of Wordware Publishing, Inc.**

From *Eyewitness to the Alamo* by Bill Groneman. Published by Republic of Texas Press, an imprint of Wordware Publishing, Inc. Copyright © 1996, Bill Groneman. Reprinted by permission.

**Simon & Schuster**

Reprinted with the permission of Simon & Schuster from *Lonesome Dove* by Larry Mc Murtry. Copyright © 1985 by Larry Mc Murtry.

**Southern Methodist University, DeGolyer Library**

"Tejanos' Petition to the Mexican Government" from *Troubles in Texas, 1832*, edited by David J. Weber and translated by Conchita Hassell Winn and David J. Weber. Published by the Wind River Press, Dallas, Texas. Copyright 1983 by the DeGolyer Library of Southern Methodist University, Dallas.

**Luci Tapahonso**

"I Am Singing Now" from *A Breeze Swept Through* by Luci Tapahonso. Copyright © 1987 Luci Tapahonso. Used by permission of the author.

**Texas Christian University Press**

"How I Won the War" by Robert Flynn from *Living with the Hyenas: Short Stories* by Robert Flynn. Copyright © 1995 Robert Flynn. Reprinted, courtesy of Texas Christian University Press.

**Thunder's Mouth Press**

"Remember" from the book *She Had Some Horses* by Joy Harjo. Copyright © 1983 by Thunder's Mouth Press. Appears by permission of the publisher, Thunder's Mouth Press.

**University of Arizona Press**

"The Snakeman" from *Sáanil Dahataal: The Women Are Singing*. Copyright © 1993 by Luci Tapahonso. Reprinted by permission of the University of Arizona Press.

**Tino Villanueva**

"Haciendo Apenas la Recolección" from *Shaking Off the Dark* by Tino Villanueva (Arte Publico Press). Copyright © 1980 Tino Villanueva. Reprinted by permission of the author.

**Albert Whitman & Company**

"Pecos Bill Discovers He Is a Human" from *Pecos Bill: The Greatest Cowboy of All Time* by James Cloyd Bowman, copyright © 1937, 1964 by Albert Whitman & Company. Used with permission of the publisher.

**Bryan Woolley**

"Hanging Around the Alamo" from *The Time of My Life* by Bryan Woolley. Copyright © 1984 by Bryan Woolley. Reprinted by permission of the author.

**The Wylie Agency, Inc.**

"Love Poem" by Leslie Marmon Silko. Copyright © 1994 by Leslie Marmon Silko, first printed in *Laguna Woman*. Reprinted with the permission of The Wylie Agency, Inc.

# Acknowledgments

**Yale University Press**
  "A Teenage Bride on the Santa Fe Trail" from *Down the Santa Fe Trail and Into Mexico: The Diary of Susan Shelby Magoffin, 1846-1847*, edited by Stella M. Drumm. Copyright © 1962. Reprinted by permission of the publisher, Yale University Press.